KEY TO

APPLIED ENGLISH GRAMMAR *and* COMPOSITION

KEY TO

APPLIED ENGLISH
GRAMMAR *and* COMPOSITION

Some more Essays on **Current Topics**
Paragraphs on **Proverbs** and **Situational Topics**
with **Key** to Grammar EXERCISES

Dr P C Das

MA, BT, DELT, PhD

New Central Book Agency (P) Ltd

LONDON

HYDERABAD ERNAKULAM BHUBANESWAR

NEW DELHI KOLKATA PUNE GUWAHATI

NCBA

REGD OFFICE
8/1 Chintamoni Das Lane, Kolkata 700 009, India
email: ncbapvtltd@eth.net

OVERSEAS
NCBA (UK) Ltd, 149 Park Avenue North, Northampton, NN3 2HY, UK
email: ncbauk@yahoo.com

EXPORT
NCBA Exports Pvt. Ltd, 212 Shahpur Jat, New Delhi 110 049
email: ncbaexports@ncbapvtltd.com

BRANCHES

2/27 Ansari Road, 1st Floor
Daryaganj, **New Delhi** 110 002
email: ncbadel@ncbapvtltd.com

House No. 3-1-315, 1st Floor
Nimboliadda, Kachiguda, **Hyderabad** 500 027
email: ncbahydb@ncbapvtltd.com

Shop Nos. 3 & 4, Vinayak Towers
681/B Budhwar Peth, Appa Balwant Chowk
Pune 411 002
email: ncbapune@ncbapvtltd.com

GSS Shopping Complex, 1st Floor
Opposite College Post Office, Convent Road
Ernakulam 682 035
email: ncbaernk@ncbapvtltd.com

Shop No. 15, Bharati Towers, Ground Floor
Forest Park, **Bhubaneswar** 751 001
email: ncbabub@ncbapvtltd.com

Radhamayee Complex (Second Floor)
Opp. SBI, Panbazar, Jaswanta Road
Guwahati 781 001
email: ncbaguwahati@ncbapvtltd.com

KEY TO APPLIED ENGLISH GRAMMAR AND COMPOSITION • P C Das

First Published: January 2013
Reprinted: January 2014
Reprinted: March 2016

PUBLISHER AND TYPESETTER
New Central Book Agency (P) Ltd
8/1 Chintamoni Das Lane, Kolkata 700 009

PRINTER
New Central Book Agency (P) Ltd
Web-Offset Division, Dhulagarh, Sankrail, Howrah

COVER PRINTER
Techno Process, Kolkata

PROOF CHECKING
Subas Maitra

PROJECT TEAM
Pradip Das, Pradip Biswas, Prodip Baidya

ISBN 978 81 7381 808 0

Price ₹ 95.00

PREFACE

I am pleased to present the ***Key to Applied English Grammar and Composition*** with the solutions of Grammar Exercises in order to help the students in checking the correct answers in the relevant topics.

Many more essays on current topics, paragraphs on proverbs, and situational topics have also been added in this booklet.

My endeavour will be amply rewarded if the students concerned feel benefitted in preparing their lessons in the field of learning English as a foreign language.

01.10.2012 **P C Das**

CONTENTS

CHAPTERS

SOME MORE ESSAYS ON CURRENT TOPICS
PARAGRAPHS ON PROVERBS
AND
SITUATIONAL TOPICS

SOME MORE ESSAYS ON CURRENT TOPICS

Here are some important Essays on current topics, Paragraphs on proverbs and Situational topics.

1. GLOBAL WARMING

Introduction : climate behaving in erratic manner—adverse effect in course of life all over the world

Causes of Global Warming : increasing volumes of emitting lethal gases due to industrial revolution, etc.—lack of public consciousness

Consequences : ice cover in the Arctic region and glaciers slowly melting—rising of water-levels in the oceans and seas—large parts of land in coastal countries may be submerged—Mt. Everest is losing its height—some species of flora and fauna may disappear—average temperature of the earth will go up—monsoon rains will be whimsical

The UN initiative : 1992 Earth Summit—Kyoto Agreement in 1997—lack of the desired will and power of the UN to control the situation

Conclusion : public awareness and urgent steps to be taken by the developed and developing countries and the UN

●

In recent times, climate has been behaving in erratic manner. And for that, unusual and unprecedented natural calamities have been adversely affecting the course of our life all over the world. It has been attributed to the phenomenon of global warming.

The vital cause of global warming is the rapid increase in volumes of emitting lethal gases, called greenhouse gases. Some of the gases in this category are carbon monoxide, carbon dioxide, methane and nitrous oxide which are highly toxic. These gases are being indiscriminately emitted by industrial activities in the developed and developing countries. The proportion has been gradually alarming since the Industrial Revolution since 1760s and has gained momentum by the end of the 20th century. Lack of public consciousness is another cause of this global threat.

Consequently, ice in the Arctic Region is now slowly melting and losing the volume by 7% per year. Glaciers are also melting gradually. Water levels in the oceans and seas will rise alarmingly and large parts of land in coastal countries may be submerged in near future. A Chinese survey has revealed the fact that the world's highest peak Mt. Everest (8,848 metres) is gradually losing its height—nearly 0.1 metre annually. Most of the glaciers in the Himalyan region may also be dry and some perennial rivers may be reduced to seasonal rivulets! Many species of flora and fauna may also disappear from the planet within two or three decades!! Average temperature of the earth will go up gradually and monsoon rains will be whimsical.

The UN is trying to tackle this grave concern. The 1992 Earth Sumit was held in Rio de Janeiro in order to take some steps to mitigate that problem. Subsequently an international agreement was negotiated in Kyoto, Japan in 1997, to control the situation. But unfortunately, lack of the desired will and power of the UN has become an impediment to reach the desired goal.

In such circumstances, public awareness should be roused by arranging seminars, etc. The press and the TV channels should also come forward. Urgent steps by the developed and developing countries and the UN are the pressing need of the day.

2. DISASTER MANAGEMENT

Introduction : two types of disaster—(a) natural, (b) accidental or man-made

Examples of Disasters : (a) man-made, (b) brought by nature

Measures to be taken : (a) post-disaster management, (b) pre-disaster steps

Role of mass media : (a) warning about an impending disaster, (b) making bridge between the victims and the aid-giving agencies, (c) public call for raising fund to help the victims

Role of Government : (a) constitution of disaster management bodies or task force, (b) preparing suitable plans, (c) training to common people to meet emergency situations; (d) relief and rehabilitation of the victims

Roll of NGOs : Ramakrishna Mission, Bharat Sevashram Sangha and other NGOs may take a vital role in such situations

●

Disaster may come in two ways. It may be natural, or it may be accidental or man-made. Earthquakes, tsunami, landslides, cyclones, floods and droughts are natural disasters. And, the collapse or catching fire of a building, train or plane accident, explosion of a bomb causing casualties, etc. are accidental or man-made disasters.

The people of Bhopal are still suffering from the tragic consequences of the Bhopal Gas Tragedy which was man-made. As to natural disasters in India, we see that Gujarat, Manipur and Arunachal are very prone to earthquake. Himachal Pradesh and Jammu and Kashmir are frequently hit by landslides. Bihar, Orissa and some parts of West Bengal are frequented with floods. Cyclones are very common in the coastal areas of Andhra Pradesh, Tamil Nadu, Kerala and West Bengal. Occasional tsunamis may also hit such areas. A large part of Rajasthan and some districts of West Bengal—such as Purulia and Bankura—suffer from drought-like conditions almost every year.

For the remedy of such disasters, measures should be taken in two broad categories—(a) post-disaster management, and (b) pre-disaster steps. Post-disaster management includes shifting the sufferers to the relief camps, providing with food, clothing and medicines, and later to rehabilitate them. But now the perspective has been extended to taking pre-disaster preventive measures too, as the proverb says—prevention is better than cure. Of course, it is not always possible to predict the exact time and magnitude of any natural disaster such as earthquake, tsunami, etc. But it is possible to take safety measures by constucting buildings,—especially in the earthquake-prone areas—in order to lessen the casualties during an earthquake. Floods may be prevented by building dams and bridges, linking more channels to rivers, and providing eco-friendly forest cover, etc. These long-term measure may help the people to face the fury of floods.

The mass media can help the people by giving timely warnings. It can act as a bridge between the sufferers and the aid-giving agencies in case of emergency. TV channels and newspapers may afford public call for raising fund to help the suffering people.

The state governments are now forming disaster management bodies or task force with skilled persons and suitable equipment. We know different disasters call for different techniques of tackling the situations. And so it is the duty of the government to prepare suitable plans for disaster management. Training should be arranged to the common people too to meet the emergency situations. Proper relief and rehabilitation should also be provided to the survivors and special care should be taken for those who are traumatised.

The Ramkrishna Mission, Bharat Sevashram Sangha and some other NGOs may also take a vital role in such situations.

3. SOCIAL NETWORKING SITES—USES AND ABUSES

Introduction : What it is—Face book; Twitter etc.

Friends and false friends : difficult to ascertain real and false friends—personal touch is lost

Illustrations : types of sites—professional oriented—private interest oriented——social interest oriented

Political impact : political e-mailing for or against an issue—uses and abuses

Conclusion : not good or bad itself—effects depend on the users

●

Social Networking Site is a Web server that allows Internet users to register themselves to create a personal profile and communicate with selected others. One can personalise one's space on this site in different ways using personal information, interests, graphics, etc. to give an idea of oneself to other people. These Social Network Websites are more and more quoted as new sources of our life including happiness, depression, addiction, and new forms of social and political life of democracy.

When we talk of friendship in the column 'friend' in these sites, we define a link that the users have with others, after a reciprocal agreement. This allows so-called 'friends' to have access to some part of the profile with personal information. Some people tend to think that 'friend' in real life has an aspect that is embedded in the private sphere of the individual, with references to reciprocity, trust and strong empathy to the other. In these sites we use summary statement of personal feelings using culturally approved terminology, and consequently the real personl touch is lost in between. A teenager faces serious problems in understanding the distinction between virtual and real friendship. However, it is been observed that most people use these media to stay connected with the people that they are already acquainted with in the Facebook conversation.

There are several types of social networking sites, such as—Facebook, My space, Twitter, Blog, Flickr, etc. Some of them are professional oriented, for example, LinkedIn, Viadeo or Xing. Their aim is to create a set of relationship and feedbacks to help both the flexibility of employers and the employees who can forward their resumé as well as ask for recommendations from their ex-employers through these sites. There are some others that are interest-oriented, for example, Flickr, a Nobi, devian Art, Live Journal. Here users are usually linked by common interests as photography, digital arts, writings, etc. Then there are social-oriented networking, for example Facebook, Orkut, My Space, Badoo, Netlog, Blog, Friendster, twitter. With these sites one can trace the activities of one's friends, chat, have a look at their profile, share pictures with others, link music, post articles or videos and comment on people's profiles.

There is another important aspect of networking site, that is, political networking. By this site one can supervise some political action and demonstrate political oriented e-mailing. It can have a positive outcome where one can fight against corruption (e.g. India Against Corruption movement led by Anna Hazare and his team). It can have negative impacts as well, like the incident in the recent past when a large number of people of North-eastern India, who live in Bangalore, were threatened to leave the city through the socio-political website and bulk SMS services, even by imposing fake photos of earthquakes of some other places. Such ethnic threats could spread like fire through these media where people are all inter-connected to one another. Consequently, some motivated incidents posted to such media could adversely affect a lot of people who are part of these electronic network.

The exponential growth of popularity of social networking sites indicates that more and more people are attracted to such sites for both personal and professional purposes. It is true that there are uses and abuses of such media. Nonetheless, it depends on who used it how. Technology itself is neither good nor bad. It is the intention of the user that will determine whether it will fetch good or bad results.

4. CYBER CRIMES

Introduction : Cyber Crimes creeping with the rise of information technology in the 21st century

Types of Cyber Crimes : (a) individual targets, (b) computer networks and devices at large

Common Cyber Crimes : (a) e-mail spoofing and spamming, (b) spreading hatred and harassment, (c) fraud, (d) drug trafficking, (e) computer terrorism, (f) online gambling, etc.

Preventive measures : (a) strict laws prohibiting cyber crimes, (b) cyber scrutiny and regular upgrading, (c) spreading awareness

●

We know every age has its peculiar progress and drawbacks. In the 21st century we see the amazing advancement in computer science as well as the crimes related to it.

Cyber Crimes or computer-related crimes are now dominating the modern crime world. It may be categorised in two broad types—(a) individual targets, and (b) computer networks and devices at large. In the first type the target may be an individual or an organization and the network acts as a facilitator. And in the second type the network itself is the target. Spreading computer viruses falls in this category.

There are some common cyber crimes such as e-mail spoofing and spamming, fraud, drug trafficking, computer terrorism, online gambling, etc. E-mail spoofing refers to such unfair affair where an e-mail from one source appears to have been sent from another concealing one's identity. E-mail spamming is the practice of sending unwanted advertising materials by e-mails.

Spreading hatred and harassment through internet is another type of cyber crime. The abuser may post blasphemous, libellous, slanderous, pornographic or seditious materials on a website. Cyber crime of fraud includes bank fraud, identity fraud, and data theft. Drug trafficking is also increasing through internet. Cyber terrorism may be committed through the use of cyber space or computer reasources. A false propaganda of an explosion of bomb, etc. in a train or a market place for creating panic or a real attack through a computer device may be an act of such cyber terrorism. Online gambling is also prevalent as a cyber crime nowadays.

Some preventive measures should be taken for internet security. More strict laws should be passed prohibiting cyber crimes. Cyber scrutiny and regular upgrading must be a routine work. Above all, awareness of the users to tighten their cyber security may help a lot to prevent or restrict cyber crimes through rapid advancement of information technology.

5. STING OPERATIONS : FOUL MEANS TO FAIR ENDS

Introduction : a necessary evil as a remedial measure for some illegal or immoral activities

Some examples : political corruption with *Tehelka* and some others—police personnel, officials of income tax, sales tax, excise, customs, health and municipal departments

Arguments for and against sting operations : (a) expose evils in the society—promote public awareness— (b) unethical operation—used to blackmail people—political parties try to settle scores with their rivals—no right to intrude into one's privacy—pervert people's taste—TV channels boost it for wide publicity

Conclusion : should be used judiciously—media should be restricted to a limit

●

A sting operation is a necessary evil as a remedial measure for some illegal or immoral activities. It is done by hidden cameras while one is engaged in any type of corruption. Now it has become quiet a craze with the people.

In our country it started with *Tehelka* when a prominent political leader was caught on camera taking a bribe. The evidence was so clear that no explanation could help him to come out clear. In another operation one was found guilty to buy MLAs for a political party. Some officers in income tax, sales tax, excise, customs, health and municipal departments were caught red-handed in sting operations. Traffic police are sometimes shown extorting money to let off the law-breaking drivers. In several jails, jail authorities are shown passing liquor bottles, mobiles, and even weapons to the hard-core criminals. Some hospital employees are shown selling life-saving drugs from hospitals. Some personnel in municipal bodies are caught involved in corruption.

However, arguments may be forwarded for and against such sting operations. Some say it exposes the evils in the society and promotes public awareness. Others say it is an unethical operation and often used to blackmail people. Sometimes political parties try to settle scores with their rivals. Not only that, in law there is no right to intrude into one's privacy. And, sometimes, it spreads the scandals and perverts the people's taste too. In most cases, the media, especially the TV channels, boost sting operations for wide publicity. And the operators who take part in sting operations may even run the risk of life to unearth the truth.

In fine, we can say that a sting operation is a powerful tool in detecting corruption and taking penal measures. But it should be used judiciously. Moreover, media should be restricted to a limit in sensational circumstances.

6. CORRUPTION IN PUBLIC LIFE
OR
CORRUPTION AND WORK CULTURE

Introduction : What is means

Present position : a deep-rooted evil in almost every walk of life — a blow to moral values

Causes of Corruption : greed for floating money—haste for getting what one wants—corruption in politics and political shelter for the law-breakers—unemployment problem aggravates the situation

Result in work culture : neglect in duties and public harassment

Measures to check corruption : individual battle may be risky—united operation—sting operation if possible—information technology and right to information—accountability in bureaucracy—political transparency

Conclusion : public awareness and moral education in schools and colleges

●

Corruption means getting something through unjustified means. We know greed is the mother of corruption and it arises from our moral weakness. Corruption includes misuse of public money for private gains, nepotism, bribery and other offences. It becomes the unholy wedlock between the bribe-giver and the bribe-taker.

Corruption is a worldwide evil and it is now deep-rooted in almost every walk of life. Some say that in our country corruption has increased like cancer after independence. According to the latest report, India is one of the 30 most-corrupt countries in the world!! And it is a blow to our moral values.

The cause of corruption lies in the greed for floating money and the haste for getting what we want. It i a shame that either in a government office or in private sector, we cannot get our work done without greasing the palms of the dealing persons. Men in power often misuse their authority. Nowadays, politics is also based on money and muscle. Political parties take forcible subscription for contesting elections. There is also the nexus between some statesmen and big business companies. Politics now stands criminalised to a great extent. Some of the political leaders often give shelters to the miscreants. They bestow undue favour in distributing licence, contracts, and permits. People give bribes which is now figuratively called 'speed money' to get their work done or to escape the law. Even the honest citizens are bound to offer bribes to obtain essential service. The unemployment situations of our country tempt the unemployed persons to get a job by any unholy means and some people exploit their needs. Corruption prevails in the lower rank and in high levels too.

The result of corruption is reflected in our work culture. The workers and employees care a little for their service rules. Sometimes the employees in the offices harass people without any reason. The offenders often escape for their political shelter. For decades they have been trained to aim their guns at the employers. They neglect their duties and become vocal and sometimes violent about their demands and rights. They should remember that rights and duties are always under one umbrella.

And in such a situation some measures must be taken to check corruption. Individual attempt against corruption may be valiant and worthy of admiration, but it cannot be sufficient to break the bastions of immorality. It may also be risky for an individual. What we mostly need is united operation. Information technology and the Right to Information Act can help us a lot to cut down red tapism. Sting operations in some cases may be effective. All these efforts can ensure accountability in bureaucracy and political transparency to a great extent.

To conclude, we must say that the way to fight against corruption is the strong and determined will of an individual and society at large. Moral education should be imparted in schools and colleges too. But the most effective way is to arouse public contempt and grow social awareness that can protect us from the cancer of corruption in our country.

7. VIOLENCE AGAINST WOMEN IN INDIA

Introduction : patriarchal society and general position of women in India

Forms of violence against women : maltreatment for dowry—physical outrage for snatching ornaments—sexual harassment and rape—eve-teasing

How to check such violence : role of social workers and NGOs—restraint on movies and TV channels showing too much sex and violence—role of women's organizations

Conclusion : more strict laws—movies and TV channels—role of women's organizations—public awareness

●

We must admit that our society is basically patriarchal and is being dominated by males. We may now claim the credit of constitutional equality between men and women but the bitter reality is that we have to go a long way to establish a safe and honourable position of women in our society. We may see some bright exceptions, but that is not sufficient to shatter the stronghold of male dominance. In general, the dignity of women has not been uniformly and continuously maintained in our country.

One of the most inhuman practices of our society is the dowry system. It turns the brides into a saleable commodity like cattle in the market of marriage! Her sufferings do not cease even with the ceremony of marriage. In many cases, the young brides are tortured or pushed to suicide or homicide by the husbands and the in-laws so that the grooms can marry anew for a dowry larger than before!!

Physical assault on women is also frequent in our day-to-day life. Many illiterate and uncultured brutes beat their wives as they are weak, helpless creatures. At fairs and festivals, in crowded places, and in the buses the lynx-eyed brutes carry on irritation and physical assault on the weaker sex.

The ladies who bear some yellow metal become the easy prey of the miscreants, especially the chain-snatchers. It is often heard that thwarted lovers mutilate their lady-love's face by throwing acid bulbs, etc. Greed of money or frustration in love is not the only motivating force behind the crimes against women. Sex hunger is another vital point. Young girls are sometimes cheated and blackmailed into a life of vice. This is the story of a lot of women in the red-light areas of various cities. Molestation and rape is another tragedy of women. Sexual harassment also occur in the offices or in working places, mostly in the night shifts. If we want to feel the urge to stop this nuisance of our social milieu, we have to know the experiences of the working women from the starting bus stop to the place of their work where they are the objects of the vulture eyes of the males. Eve-teasing on the streets is also an indirect violence on women.

If this trend has to be checked, more strict laws should be activated. Our social workers and NGOs should come forward to form public awareness. Moreover, there should be some restraints on movies and TVs showing too much sex and violence. The obscene hoardings should also be banned. Finally, the women's organizations themselves should shoulder much of the responsibility to check violence against women in our society.

8. TERRORISM IN THE WORLD AND IN INDIA

Introduction : What is it?

Causes of terrorism : political frustration, religious and racial fanaticism—economic backwardness—external powers that encourage terrorism

Hot fields : Iraq, Iran, Afganistans, Sri Lanka, USA, and in India—Jammu and Kashmir, Tamil Nadu, Maharashtra, Assam, Nagaland, Mijoram, and Tripura

Manifestations in India : kidnapping, hijacking. sabotage, murder of political leaders—shooting down innocent people—blasting bombs, etc.

Prominent groups : ULFA in Assam, LTTE in Tamil Nadu, Maoists in Andhra Pradesh, Chhatisgarh, Orissa, Bihar, Jharkhand and parts of West Bengal

Evil effects of terrorism : strikes at the roots of democracy—obstructs economic development—creates insecurity in the minds of the people

Meeting the challenge : anti-terrorist squads—public cooperation—negotiation to bring the terrorists to the mainstream of national life

Conclusion : maintaining law and order with simultaneous negotiation

●

The literal meaning of the word 'terrorism' is "the use of violence and intimidation, especially for political purposes". But nowadays terrorism is being used as a violent tactics for many purposes all over the world. We see that through terrorism individuals, groups or communities are applying violent actions against innocent people to elicit their support or compel the government to yield to their demands—however ant-inational or anti-constitutional they may be. The attacks on the World Trade Centre in the USA was an international horror.

The causes of terrorism are political furstration, religious and racial fanaticism. Sometimes economic backwardness of the people in an area aggravates them. And sometimes external powers such as ISI, Laskar-i-Taiba etc. encourage terrorism. The hot fields of operation are Iraq, Iran, Afganistan, Pakistan, Sri Lanka, USA, and in India—Jammu and Kashmir, Tamil Nadu, Maharashtra, Assam, Nagaland, Mijoram, and Tripura.

The violent tactics adopted by the terrorists are sometimes for personal gains when a child or a woman is kidnapped and kept for ransom. Sometimes it is in the form of hijacking of aeroplanes, sabotage, murder of political leaders or shooting down innocent people or blasting bombs in a train or a bus or a crowded area like railway stations, supermarkets, etc.

The prominent groups of terrorists in India are ULFA in Assam, LTTE in Tamil Nadu and Maoists in Andhra Pradesh, Chhattisgarh, Orissa, Bihar, Jharkhand and in Jangal Mahal in West Bengal.

Terrorists do not usually believe that problems can be solved through discussions across the table. They try to force the government to concede their demands at gunpoint. Thus terrorism strikes at the very root of democracy. It also obstructs economic development and creates insecurity in the minds of people.

It is difficult to come in terms with the terrorists as there is no unity among different groups. Besides, negotiations are hampered with forced surrender. Anti-terrorist squads may be strengthened to meet the challenge, but they will not be able to eradicate the menace without public cooperation.

Though all attempts must be taken to curb terrorism by enforcing law and order through military and paramilitary forces, negotiations should also be done simultaneously to bring the terrorists to the mainstream of national life. Besides, some international efforts should also be taken with utmost sincerity to put an end to such inhuman practice of terrorism.

9. COMMUNAL HARMONY OR SECULARISM

Introduction : Co-existence of all communities in peace and amity—getting equal or proportionate opportunities of development and sharing each other's socio-religious pattern in a multi-lingual and multi-racial state

Contemporary trends of disintegration: political, linguistic, regional and economic problem—religious fanaticism—communalism for narrow political gains —terrorist activities

Remedial measures : strict secular policy of the government—responsibility of the communal leaders—role of the mass media—public awareness—moral education in school and college syllabus

●

Communal harmony or secularism means co-existence of all communities in peace and amity. It implies that all communities should get equal or proportionate opportunities of development and sharing each other's socio-religious pattern in a multi-lingual and multi-racial state. It is the essential condition of attaining progress of any multi-religious country.

In 1947 India emerged as a secular state. Our Constitution says that our state is not identified with any particular religion. But the separatist tendencies are very active at present. There are political, linguistic, regional and economic problems. Religious fanaticism and communalism for narrow political gains aggravate the situation. While there are poverty, starvation, illiteracy and unemployment, the Mandir-Masjid issue should not come to the forefront. The demolition of Babri Masjid added to the gravity of the situation. The communal strife with vested interests in Gujarat was a shocking incident. It was really a blow to the peace-loving citizens. The reservation policy for Scheduled Castes and Tribes and the backward classes has added flame to the fire in different communities. Thus the disruptive forces of casteism, communalism, inter-State differences and parochialism have begun to raise their ugly heads to threaten the country's unity. Then there is the problem of terrorist activities. The problem of the Naga and the Mizo rebels and the Gorkhaland issues are a serious headache to the nation. The situations in Assam, Jammu and Kashmir, and the Maoist activities in different parts of the country are throwing a challenge to the unity of our nation. Our politicians and anti-social elements exploit the situation by fanning the fire.

It is ironical that we are advocating the concepts of international peace while we are unable to eliminate communalism in our own country. If two communities cannot co-exist, how can two nations?

At this juncture some remedial measures must be taken. The government must follow a strictly secular policy and help to develop each community impartially. Maximum responsibility lies with religious and communal leaders not to generate hatred, but tolerance. Our political leaders should give up the politics of vote-bank and work in greater national interest. The role of the media should be unbiased and without communal colouring. Moral education should be emphasised in school and college syllabus. Above all, public awareness should be the active force to preserve peace and amity among different communities in order to maintain the secular character of the country.

10. POPULATION EXPLOSION AND FAMILY PLANNING

Introduction : global problem—population alarming in India

Magnitude of the problem : comparison between India and advanced countries of the West

Evil effects of over-population : food problem—malnutrition—unemployment—greater pressure on land—imbalance in the growth of economy—deforestation and problem of ecological balance—high pollution levels—overcrowding of cities and increasing slums—high crime rate in cities—low standard of living

Family planning programme : governmental planning—religious prejudice and ignorance—early marriage—wrong notions about contraceptives—effect in urban and rural areas

Measures to be taken : mass education, especially women's education—role of mass media—further planning of the government—public awareness

●

Population explosion is a global problem. Of course, 'over-population', is a relative term. The density of population per square mile is about 350 in India, while it is about only 41 per square mile in the USA. Thus over-population is assuming an alarming proportion in India.

If we compare the situation with the advanced countries of the West, we can feel the magnitude of the problem. Next to China, India is the most densely populated country in the world. According to the latest census report in 2011 the population of the country is about 120 crore. Here the average annual rate of population growth is 4.5% while it is about 0.5% in the advanced Western countries. Thus every two years India adds some 25 million people to its numbers, that is more than the total population of Canada. The average lifespan has also increased because of better preventive medicines, public health and hygienic measures, and a considerable drop in infant mortality. Moreover, a part of the pressure of population in India is due to the influx of refugees from Pakistan (1947 on) and Bangladesh (1971 on). All these have led to the pressure of population in our country.

The evil effects of over-population in India are too many. Food and accommodation are the foremost. Instead of becoming a national asset, the growth of population has become a national liability. Whatever is gained in terms of economic growth is neutralised by the rising numbers. More children do not mean more workers of the future, but more people without work, more mouths to feed. And, therefore, the expenditure per capita is bound to be less. The poor people care a little how to bring up the children properly. They do not care at all for their education. Though the government has adopted a series of plans for economic development, the growth of population has upset all the plans. The result is the poor are burdened with more poverty, more hunger, more distress and disease. The fate is not only malnutrion and unemployment, but greater pressure on land, imbalance in the growth of economy, deforestation and the problem of ecological imbalance. It is creating overcrowding of cities, increasing slums, high pollution level, high rate of crime in cities—and overall low standard of living.

India adopted family planning in 1952 and has been carrying it out through Five-Year Plans. But it has not achieved the expected success. Though it has earned some effect on the urban population, the rural population, at large, remain untouched. The factors of failure are mainly religious prejudice, ignorance, early marriage and wrong notions about contraceptives, etc. Family planning in also opposed by the orthodox Muslims though the progressive section feels its urgent need. Hence some measures must be taken to control the population on war footing. More stress should be laid on mass education, especially women's education. Early marriage before adulthood must be stopped. The most important step is to motivate the masses to adopt family planning. The government should take immediate steps to further the planning. The mass media, especially TVs, can play a vital role in spreading the family planning programme with useful information. Above all, urgent and earnest public awareness is the pressing need.

11. PROBLEM OF UNEMPLOYMENT

Introduction : a major problem all over the world, especially in India

Present state of unemployment : unemployed persons in urban areas—unemployed population in rural areas—pseudo-employment far bigger than the registered number in Employment Exchanges

Causes of unemployment : over-population—defective system of education—lack of coordination between educational planning and job-seeking programmes—industrial unrest leading to lock-outs and lay-offs

Effects of unemployment : breeds frustration and anti-social activities—poor standard of living—brain drain

Government programmes : Prime Minister's Rozgar Yojana—Swarna Jayanti Yojana in urban areas—Gram Swarozgar Yojana, Jawahar Gram Samridhi Yojana and Employment Assurance scheme in rural areas

Other measures : controlling the growth of population—more vocational education—more self-employment

Conclusion : self-help is the best help

●

Unemployment is a problem all over the world. But that cannot be our consolation. Today India faces it in its serious form. The number of unemployed youths in our country has already reached an alarming proportion; and still the number is increasing every year. It is really a matter of pity and shame that, though willing to work, a large number of our youths find no scope of employment.

In fact, unemployment is not only a curse, but it is worse than a disease. It weakens the body and mind and eats up the vitality of our young population. We must admit that every man and women should have ample scope of employment. It is his or her birthright. But unfortunately, in our country there are more people than jobs. Thousands of young people remain idle even after completing their studies in both urban and rural areas. Their number is far bigger than the registered number in Employment Exchanges. Moreover, there are unemployed millions in rural areas, and pseudo-employment having only seasonal work.

We should analyse the causes behind such alarming situation. The most important factor is the rapid growth of population. We see that the population is growing fast, but there is no expansion of corresponding avenues of employment. Our system of education is also defective. It is not satisfactorily related to the socio-economic needs of our people. This lack of coordination between educational planning and job-seeking programmes is aggravating the problem. Automation and insufficiency of side-avenues are also becoming great factors for increasing unemployment. Industrial unrest has also led to lock-outs and lay-offs throwing the workers out of employment.

Thus the situation is growing worse and gradually slipping out of control. Some of our angry youngmen turn to be anti-social out of their frustration, and some others lead an idle life. Ultimately, this leads to our poor standard of living. And some talented youths migrate to foreign countries and we helplessly see such brain-drain.

Of course, there are some government programmes to control the unemployment problem, such as —Prime Minister's Rozgar Yojana, Swarna Jayanti Yojana in urban areas, Gram Swarozgar Yojana, Jawahar Gram Samridhi Yojana and Employment Assurance Scheme by giving job cards from Panchayets in rural areas.

There must be some other measures too. And among them controlling the growth of population is the most important. More vocational education can offer greater employment opportunities to our youths. By reviving the cottage and small-scale industries, we can also solve the problem of rural unemployment. More self-employment should also be provided with the assistance of the banks. However, no one can deny the bitter and bare fact that no government can provide employment for all unemployed youths. So we should change our notion of a secure and comfortable job with a chair and a table and a fan overhead in an office or in a bank. We must follow the principle—"Self-help is the best help".

12. VOCATIONAL EDUCATION

Introduction : What it means—why so important—comparison with other advance countries

Fields of Vocational Education : fields befitting average students—agriculture, horticulture, carpentry, pottery, tailoring, book-binding, spinning, weaving, dairy, poultry, etc.—paraprofessional courses, such as printing, tourism, hotel management, photography, stagecraft, basic computer, commercial publicity, journalism, etc.

Conclusion : some branches of vocational education not up to the mark—should be a reality-based planning—government policy of different grades of institutes for different levels of students.

●

Vocational education is a training that enables a man to earn his bread by pursuing a profession in life. It is specially important in the context of the economic realities of the country at present. The problem of unemployment has assumed alarming situations. No government can provide employment to all the unemployed youths. In all technically advanced countries like England, America, Russia, Germany, China, Japan — only the selected talents are encouraged to go up for higher education in general stream. The majority of youngmen have to attend a preparatory school, and then some vocational schools. Under such circumstances, vocational education is preferable to the traditional one for a large section of students in our country.

All men are not equally gifted, but the basic needs of all men are the same. Hence our boys and girls should receive training in certain crafts according to their aptitude and ability. There are so many branches of vocational education for the common students such as — agriculture, horticulture, carpentry, pottery, tailoring, book-binding, spinning, weaving, dyeing, dairy, poultry, etc. Such vocational training can be a powerful means of combating unemployment which is looming large in our country. It can be a means of steady supply of skilled hands to different productive centres as well as it can provide the scope for self-employment too. Besides fully vocational institutions, our schools and colleges can be partly vocationalised with paraprofessional courses, such as printing, tourism, hotel management, photography, stagecraft, basic computer, commercial publicity, journalism, etc. And then it will open new avenues of employment before the young generation and save them from frustration.

It is true that unfortunately even some branches of vocational education are not up to the mark in manpower recruitments resulting in unemployment even among vocationally trained students. So there should be reality-based planning of vocational eduction as per requirements which may be different in different States. Still we must admit that there is a wider scope for expansion of centres of vocational education even in upper classes of High and Higher Secondary schools in our country. The government should, therefore, take more effective steps to establish different grades of institutes for the students of different levels for their vocational education.

13. REALITY SHOWS ON TV

Introduction : recent innovations of Indian television — a catchy event

Basic features : a participative role of the audition through the voting system — an emotional chord

Impact of reality shows : opportunities for young aspirants to have a show of their talents — TV channels gain popularity and advertisement

Problems : too much involvement leads to physical and mental pressure — children are robbed of their free childhood

Conclusion : a mixture dish of good and bad—doubts about the authenticity of the voting system, the method of selection, etc.

●

Reality show is the recent innovation on Indian television. It is a catchy event based on new 'out-of-the box' ideas.

Such reality shows have two basic features. The first is an interaction with the audience having a participative role through the voting system. Secondly, it serves great influence on our emotional chord which is no less a cause of its success.

Reality shows give opportunities for young aspirants to have a show of their talents on TV channels. Thus both the aspirants and the TV channels gain popularity and wide publicity including lucrative advertisements. Shows 'Sa Re Ga Ma Pa' on Zee TV, 'EK phone EK Lakh' on Channel 10, etc. encourage to dream and assist to turn their dreams into reality.

However, reality shows bring with them some problems as well. The viewers who very often get glued to watch these shows become addicted to it. Sometimes it is both painful and ludicrous to see the stage-managed agreements and disagreements, cheers and tears on the screen. Too much involvement leads to physical and mental pressure on both the viewers and the participants. Children who are engaged in such reality shows are often diverted from their regular studies. Long hours of practice, provocative dances and dresses, and demeaning gestures often rob the children of their childhood. Even those who watch these shows may be tempted to behave or speak likewise or even try dangerous stunts accordingly. Thus the reality shows may exert a negative impact on their soft minds. Hence several organizations that uphold child rights, protest against the involvement of children in such reality shows.

To conclude, we must say that these reality shows are a mixture of good and bad dishes. Moreover, such reality shows have come under a lot of criticism as they sometimes bear doubts about the authenticity of the voting system, the method of selecting the winners and the reality behind the so-called reality shows.

14. EXAMINATION—A NECESSARY EVIL

Introduction : an integral pat of our system of education but not flawless— perhaps evil, yet indispensable on the point of evaluation

Arguments for holding examination: examinations compel students to study— essential for evaluation—bright students make bright results, poor ones make poor results—may not be cent percent accurate, still carry substantial justice

Arguments against holding examination : role of chance—encourage cramming — enjoy a ten-month idleness and have a two-month strenuous work—affects class teaching

Suggestions for reforms : evaluation throughout the year—semester system should be introduced—balance between objective-type questions and essay-type questions—leakage of question papers should be checked—standard of invigilation should be improved—scripts should be examined by the examiners of proven ability under strict supervision of head examiner—scope of reviewing if wanted

Conclusion : in absence of examinations students would not study at all—in spite of all the drawbacks, a good student does not usually fail or a backward student does not come to the top list—a necessary evil having no other better alternative

●

Examination is an integral part of our system of education, though it is not flawless. They are perhaps evil, yet they are indispensable on the point of evaluation.

There are arguments for and against holding examinations in our institutions. Those who argue for the system say that examinations compel the students to study the syllabus. It is essential for evaluation of the performance of the students. We see that bright students make bright results and poor ones cut a sorry figure in the examinations. Moreover, the system of examination may not be cent percent accurate, still it carries some substantial justice.

However there are some arguments against the system. The opposers say that there is a very prominent role of chance instead of justice in the results of examinations. In their opinion marking varies in the hands of difficult examiners. Even it differs in case of one examiner at different moments. An educationist once said humorously that marking varies before dinner and after dinner. Moreover, the present system of examination encourages cramming instead of assimilation of the subject matters. And the students, at large, enjoy a ten-month idleness and have a two-months' strenuous work for being prepared for the examination. Class teaching is also hampered in this system in two ways. An ideal teacher finds himself limited in teaching in the boundary for preparing the students to score good marks only. And some students feel bored in the class and abstain from attendance.

Some suggestions for reforms of the system may be offered in this context. Evaluation should be done throughout the year instead of a few days only scheduled for the examination. The whole course should be divided into a number of semesters. There should be a balance between the objective-type questions and thought-provoking essay-type questions. Leakage of question papers should also be checked. Standard of invigilation should be improved in the examination hall. Answer scripts should be such that it reduces probability of casual marking and the temptation of earning more money by doing a hurried job. Above all, the scope of reviewing the answer scripts before a student should be allowed, if wanted.

To conclude, we must say that in absence of examinations, students would not study at all. We cannot deny that examinations have some evil effects. But even the devil must be given its due. And we must admit that in spite of all the drawbacks a good student does not usually fail or a backward student does not come to the toplist. Hence the system of examination is a necessary evil having no other better alternative.

15. RIGHTS AND DUTIES OF A CITIZEN

OR

LIBERTY IS NOT A PERSONAL AFFAIR ONLY BUT A SOCIAL CONTRACT

Introduction : unrestrained liberty means anarchy—a citizen has some rights as well as some responsibilities too

Rights of a citizen : right of protection of one's life and property, freedom of speech, etc.—right to exercise franchise to elect a government

Full liberty in private life : full liberty in one's personal choice—what to eat, what to read, what religion to practice, etc.

Living not merely for self, but for society : One's liberty should be restrained to accommodate other's—participating in public life—serving the fellow-citizens of the country

Laws essential for the preservation of liberty : laws to regulate liberty—no laws, no liberty

Conclusion : rights and duties of laws and liberty go hand in hand

●

The champions of liberty vehemently oppose any limitation on individual liberty. They do not understand that unrestrained liberty actually leads to anarchy. A citizen has some rights given by a State, and, at the same time, he has to take some responsibilities too.

A citizen should have the right of protection of his life and property, freedom of speech, etc. He should also have the right to exercise franchise to elect a government. A person should have full liberty in his private life, such as in one's personal choice — what to eat, what to read, what religion to practice.

On the other hand, he must have some duties to his fellowmen and to the State. So one's liberty should be restrained to accommodate others, for liberty is not a personal affair only, but a social contract. John Stuart Mill gives a very apt remark : "The liberty of the individual must be thus far limited, he must not make himself a nuisance to other people." The State claims something from us as we owe something to a State. So the essential qualities of a citizen are to be aware of both his rights and duties. A citizen is a member of a civilised society of a State. So he has to abide by some rules of the society. His life is not only for self, but also for the society. So he should participate in public life and serve the fellow-citizens of the country. Primarily, every citizen must be loyal to his country or State.

Laws are essential to regulate liberty, or, we can otherswise say — no laws, no liberty. For example, the traffic rules do not deny the liberty of the driver to drive his vehicle, but regulate the traffic to ensure smooth and danger-free movement and avoid traffic jam. A citizen must obey the rules of the State, and not to break them or go against them. It is the duty of a citizen to pay taxes, and help as far as possible for the uplift of other fellow-citizens. So he will not remain confined in his selfish life, but he should share his responsibilities in social welfare too. Thus he should serve the State to the best of his power, even at the cost of his personal interests.

Finally, we can say that liberty is the right to do everything which the laws allow and the rights go hand in hand with duties. If a man has some rights as a citizen, he must have some obligations too. Above all, it is his duty to honour the rights of others, and not to encroach upon others' freedom in any way.

16. GENERATION GAP

Introduction : gap between the old and the young—the old think their time better—the young think the old are fools

Gap widening : lack of intimacy between the old and the young—young generation turbulent

Gap wider for globalisation : disrespect for age-old tradition—gap wide in Western countries

Remedy : efforts to bridge the gap—the old be sympathetic—the young be tolerant

●

The gap between the old and the young people in a society is called generation gap. The old have wisdom and experience, but they are sometimes irritating. On the other hand, the young people are inexperienced and impatient. Old people think that their time was better and during their times young boys and girls were more obedient, better behaved and had greater respect for their elders. They opine that lack of respect for the elder and disrespect to the traditional system of the society will bring disaster for young generation. Young boys and girls, on the other hand, think — "The old are fools." In their view, the old cannot understand the present situation and cannot welcome any change in the old system. The fact is that the dreaming youth are looking to the future, while the old folk are casting their last, lingering glance behind.

There are some prominent factors responsible for such generation gap. The way of life is now so busy and so fast that parents find little time to devote to their children. So the intimate relation between the elders and the young is getting loosened day by day. Moreover, many of the young ones are the victims of frustration for unemployment. They do not find any job when they come out of the schools or colleges. In such a situation, some of them become anti-socials and try to break the law of the land. Those who are somehow idealistic feel disgusted to find corruption in every walk of life. They become the angry generation in turn.

It is also the fact that the young generation finds it difficult to suit the age-old tradition of the country especially in the age of globalisation. To express their unhappiness and difference of opinion with the existing state of affairs, young people revolt or behave badly. They have little respect for the old traditions, customs and manners. Thus the gap between the old and the new grnerations is widening day by day. The gap is, of course, wider in the Western countries. It goes to such an extent that the old and the new generations live separately. However, in India the situation is not so worse. Though the traditional joint family system is going to break up, the old parents still live with their adult ones under one umbrella.

We must find out a remedy for the malady and a way for a golden handshake between the old and the young. In order to bridge the generation gap, the old should be more sympathetic towards the young. They should realize the emotion, ambition and problems of the young. On the other hand, the young should realize that they have no vast experience of life as the old have. So they should have a patient hearing and put much value to the advice of the old. We believe this cooperative spirit will act as a healthy tonic to build up the bond between the old and the young. A fine blend of age and youth is needed for human welfare in future.

17. FAST FOOD/JUNK FOOD—A HEALTH HAZARD

Introduction : modern life always in a hurry—looking for short-cuts even in food habit—fast food is easy to cook—convenient to take though with a long-term risk

Bad effects of fast food : hampers normal food habit—tends to be addictive—leads to obesity—promotes several disease, such as, risk of sugar, high blood pressure, cancer, hypertensions and heart disease—soft drinks lead to osteoporosis, tooth decay and damage to kidney

Fast food and children : get easily addicted—disorder in the balance of hormone secretion—malnutrition—obesity—various health hazards

Conclusion : acceptable occasionally, but not as a habit—excessive consumption must be restricted

●

Modern life is a fast life. It is always in a hurry, always looking for short-cuts for saving time and energy. It is reflected even in our food habit. We are no longer interested in a proper meal. It is much more convenient to take a pizza or a burger, an egg-roll or a dish of *Chowmin* or *Maggi*. Eat a pizza and wash it down with a Coke or a Pepsi. No messing up. No more than a few materials. Fast food is easy to cook in a short time and it is also convenient to take though it carries a long-term risk of health hazards.

But we should see the bad effects of fast food. Increased intake of fast food hampers our normal food habit and creates a vicious eycle in the body. Scientific study has exposed that fast food is usually rich in fats and salts and also high-calorie. It is so tasty and quick to finish that consuming fast food easily tends to be addictive. If one gets hooked to it, it is difficult to give it up in spite of strong warnings that it is unhealthy. The high calories, and fat taken with the fast food are piled up in the body and lead to obesity. Moreover, it promotes several diseases such as diabetes, cancer, hypertension, high blood pressure and heart disease. It may also impair the brain function, such as, lack of concentration and loss of memory. It may put undue strain on liver too. Excessive consumption of soft drinks lead to osteoporosis, tooth decay and damage to kidney.

Children in the urban areas, especially in the middle class and well-to-do families, are very fond of fast food. First, the adults introduce the children to such food; next the children get easily addicted to it, and the whole family in turn. And this food habit causes disorder in the balance of hormone secretion, malnutrition, obesity and various health harards.

Finally, we can say that fast food may be acceptable occasionally but not as a habit. And so excessive consumption of it must be restricted.

18. COMPUTER AND WE

Introduction : first appearance and later development

Structure of computer : five divisions—control, memory, maths, input and output device—recent research on 'artificial intelligence'

Different uses : banks, shops, hospitals, laboratories, railways, traffic control system, education, trade, industry, etc.—medical diagnosis—space flights—millions of calculations in a few seconds—data storing for future use—teaching computers—future prospect for receiving telephone calls, cooking food, cleaning rooms, preparing and submitting electric bills, etc.—virus problem in computer —internet

Conclusion : fear in the past—efficient service at present—opens new avenues of employment—another name of development

●

Computer is the latest miracle of science. It has brought in a revolution in almost every sphere of our modern life. It was first anticipated in 1838 when Charles Babbage designed a machine called 'Analytical Engine' to make difficult calculations and store memory. In 1946 the first computer was made. And since then it has been spreading its avenues ceaselessly. In fact, if the first half of the 20th century is the age of electricity, the second half is surely the age of computers, and after the first decade of the 21st century we see marvel after marvel of computer.

A computer has five divisions in its body—control, memory, maths, input and output device. 'Control' assures that the machine functions properly. In 'memory' section data are stored. Calculation is done in 'Maths'. 'Input device' supplies data and command to the machine. 'Output device' displays the final result in print. But one thing we must remember that computer cannot conceive itself beyond its program. Still scientists are now working on 'artificial intelligence'. The use of computer is growing fast.

At present it is widely used in many countries in the fields of banks, shop, hospitals, laboratories, railways, traffic control system, education, trade, industry, etc. In the field of medical diagnosis computers are doing wonders. The present space-flights have become possible only because of the successful operation of the computers. However, the computer not only makes millions of calculations within a few seconds, but also store data for future use. Now the records are not required to be kept in files. They can be stored in a small chip in the computer. It may help students in their studies too. In advanced countries 'teaching computers' are already available. In India too, computer courses of different levels are being introduced in schools and colleges. The days are not far behind when it will spread into masses more and more, and it will receive the telephone calls, cook our food, clean our rooms, prepare and submit electric bills, etc. However, the virus problem in computer internet is a great hazard.

There was a time when a section of people in India was against the use of computer in the offices, banks, etc. Their argument was that as the computer can do lots of jobs within a very short time, it will throw thousands of workers into unemployment. But nowadays we see that introduction of computers in selected fields is a must for efficient services. Moreover, although it is causing some unemployment, it opens up new avenues of employment.

Finally, we must say that we cannot go against time as computer is another name of development. It seems that computer is going to take charge of the future civilization of man.

19. MAN AND MACHINES

OR

TECHNOLOGY AND THE MODERN MAN

Introduction : What is technology or the art of making a complex machine

Its evolution : from Stone Age to the Age of Bronze and Iron new appliances to do wonderful things

Man's constant companion : machines serving like slaves — transport, agriculture, industry, etc. mechanised to relieve man of tiresome monotonous work

Bad effects of machines : over-dependence on machines turns man into machines — aggravates the problem of unemployment

Conclusion : the fault not of technology, but of its users—balance in man's life style

●

Now we live at the age of technology. God has blessed man with a wonderful brain, and with this brain he has invented a number of techniques. The sum total of these techniques is what we call technology or the art of making complex machines. The Oxford Reference Dictionary, however, defines technology as 'the application of scientific knowledge for practical purposes'.

The primitive man could only invent some techniques to make some useful tools made of stone. Then the age of bronze and iron appeared. And then after a long process of evolution we have got complex machines, matching the very tempo of our life.

Now at every step of life we enjoy the gifts of technology. Machines are now man's constant companion and they are serving us like slaves. They have relieved much of our stress of irksome works and made our life easy and enjoyable. Transport, agriculture, industry— all these fields have been mechanised in order to relieve man of tiresome and monotonous labour. The motor car, the train, the ships and the aeroplane have brought revolution in transport system. Agriculture was man's major occupation. Today bulk of agricultural work from tilling the land to the harvesting of crops is done with the help of machines. Industry too has been completely mechanised. Technological invention like computer has taken over plenty of work of the human brain. It has brought speed and accuracy in our work. Modern age is relying more and more on computers.

But such dependence on machine has turned man into machine. And its result is that a modern man behaves mechanically with others. Over-dependence on machines has made his heart hard and devoid of finer sentiments and his body incapable of physical labour. In the mad pursuit of material prosperity man has been gradually losing his human qualities. We see that technology has not only invented a robot, but has turned a man into a robot in some cases. Thus it has encroached upon man's mental peace and he has become a victim of stress and strain. Moreover, machines have aggravated the problem of unemployment. At present man finds it difficult to cope with the speed of technology invented by him. It is also an irony—machines that should be his slaves, have today turned him into their slaves.

But technology should not be blamed for this. It is not the fault of technology or machines, but of its users. Modern man should take up this challenge and bring a balance in his life style. Machines must not be allowed to be the masters of man robbing him of the very charms of life. We must remember that science and technology, as a whole, is a good servant, but a bad master.

20. RAGGING—AN EVIL PRACTICE

Introduction : What it means—supporters' argument for it as an ordeal to make the students fit for the future struggle of existence—an academic evil

Various forms of ragging : bathing in ice-cold water in a cold weather—passing the whole wintry night without any clothes—staring at or kissing a thousand watt bulb—walking naked along the corridor—walking on the cornice of a hostel building—crawling under a cot or a car—saying obscene words towards their sisters, etc.

Effects : giving up studies—losing mental balance and physical injuries—hospitalisation—some succumb to fatal death

Conclusion : how to stop it

●

As per Oxford Advanced Learner's Dictionary' by A. S. Hornby, 'ragging' means 'series of practical jokes on somebody, e.g. by college students'. Modern fanatics, especially in professional colleges, use it as an equivalent of 'Nabin Baran' which means a welcome to the newcomers in a very cruel form. Nowadays it has been turned to a nightmare to students and their guardians at the time of admission to Engineering, Polytechnical and Medical colleges. The supporters of ragging offer an argument that it as an ordeal to make the students fit for the future struggle for existence. Yet we must say that it is nothing but an academic evil.

Various forms of ragging are in practice in professional colleges. These are bathing in ice-cold water in a cold weather, passing the whole wintry night in the open without any clothes, staring at or kissing a thousand watt lamp, walking naked along the corridor, or walking on the cornice of a hostel building. Many fat students are compelled to crawl under a cot or a car. Some are made to say obscene words towards their sisters. All these cruel practices bring the newcomers to a breaking point of nerves and normal values.

The reports of recent incidents of ragging in some of the reputed professional colleges in our State are quite alarming. It is a matter of shame that even though ragging has been criticised for decades, we still come across such incidents of inhuman torture as throwing someone down the staircase or making someone stare at an electric bulb until one turns blind. As a result, many students give up their studies and go back home; some lose their mental balance; some are seriously injured and have to be hospitalised and some succumb to death.

Indeed, ragging has become a dreadful affair in the institutions of higher learning, especially in professional colleges. It seem to be a survival of medieval barbarism. The press and TV channels draw our notice to this cruel practice. Even the parliament of our country has taken a serious note of it. It seems that a mere appeal to one's human sensibilities and verbal criticism cannot cure this disease. It is high time that public opinion strongly asserts itself against it. The government should also pass strict laws to stop ragging and anybody found guilty of indulging in any form of ragging should be severely dealt with. We should have a clear call for the students concerned — "Welcome joys, not pain. Quit ragging."

21. AIDS—THE MOST FATAL DISEASE

Introduction : abbreviation of Acquired Immuno-Deficiency Syndrome—first detection of AIDS in America in the late 1970s—the first AIDS Day on December 1, 1992—creating consciousness

Rapid spread : number of AIDS patients about four crores all over the world—India not spared—cause of AIDS, a virus named HIV—transmitted from one to another through blood, saliva, semen, secretion from vagina, etc.

Illness and treatment : illness begins with high fever and swollen glands— recovers in two or three weeks, but relapses again vehemently—lymph nodes highly infected—WBC high and RBC low—succumb within two years and die without any effective treatment—detection by Elisa Method or Western Blot Method, very expensive.

Conclusion : prevention, the only way to fight against it—some careful measures : avoiding reckless sexual contacts, transfusion of infected blood, disallowing a diseased woman to bear a child, etc—public awareness is the pressing need—the press and the TV channels should also come forward

●

AIDS is the abbreviation of Acquired Immuno-Deficiency Syndrome. It was detected first in America in the late 1970s. The first AIDS Day was observed all over the world on the 1st December 1992. The purpose of the observance of the AIDS Day was to create consciousness about the dreadfulness of the disease and to enlighten the people on its prevention.

AIDS is an incurable disease. It has spread very rapidly and it is feared that the number of AIDS patients is about four crores all over the globe. Even India is not spared from its attack. AIDS is caused by a virus named HIV (Human Immuno-Deficiency Virus). HIV destroys the blood cells which fights the bacterial virus. In such a condition the body is totally defenceless against all kinds of infection. HIV is transmitted from one human body to another through blood, saliva, semen, secretions from vagina, etc.

An attack of AIDS begins usually with a brief illness with high fever and swollen glands. The patient recovers in two or three weeks and feels fine until he again feels sick and the disease relapses vehemently. It is now that his lymph nodes are highly infected and his WBC (white blood cell) count is very high and RBC (red blood cell) very poor. Patients succumb within two years and die without any effective treatment. No vaccine, no medicine has yet been prepared though thorough research is going on throughout the world for its prevention and cure. The detection of AIDS by Elisa Method or Western Blot Method is yet very expensive.

Prevention is the only way to fight against this dreadful disease. And for this, some measures should be taken such as — reckless sexual contacts should be avoided, transfusion of blood with HIV positive should not be done, and a diseased woman should not be allowed to bear a child, etc. AIDS poses a grave challenge to medical science as till now man is defenceless against it. Hence public awareness is the pressing need by arranging seminars etc. The press and the TV channels should also come forward for this purpose.

22. SCIENCE AND RELIGION

Introduction : scope of comparison—different fields—material world and spiritual world—Science depends on observation and reason, and religion depends on intuition and faith

Earlier conflict of science and so-called religion : confusion of religion and superstition—conflict between science and superstition, not between science and true religion

Scientific outlook : a boon not only because of its inventions, but also for giving us a scientific outlook—tangible and spectacular—universal as based on reason

Essence of religion : character, purity of heart and service to mankind

Conclusion : seeking light through different ways of science and religion

●

There can be comparison between two things when they both belong to the same category. But when they are of two different types, how can there be any comparison between them? Science deals with the objects and phenomena of external nature, religion speaks of the inner world of man. Science deals with the material world, and religion deals with the spiritual world. Science is an instrument by which man can find truth by experiments and the power of reasoning. Religion is a process of being and becoming pure in heart through realization by intuition and faith. We need both science and religion for our body and soul. And so Albert Einstein once said, "Science is lame without religion, and religion without science is blind."

We often confuse religion with superstition. It is sometimes said that Bruno, Galileo and Copernicus stood against religion for promoting science even at the cost of their lives. No, they stood against superstition, not religion. The beauty and strength of Christianity lies in the Sermon, not in the theory of creation. Even if all the theories in the Bible be exploded, real Christianity is safe; the message of Jesus will inspire people everywhere in the world irrespective of colour and creed. It is the same with every other religion.

Science is a boon to human civilization, not only for its various inventions, but also for giving us a scientific outlook. It is tangible and spectacular. It is also universal as it is based on reason. It commands so much confidence because in science everything is above board. It does not recognize any privileged individual or class. Nowadays most men will go to the doctors rather than to the Church Fathers when taken ill. When a modern man finds that his forefathers depended on priests for such ailments which he himself can now easily cure, his faith in religion is rudely shaken. Why pray to God for curing your illness when a simple dose of medicine can cure you? But here too we tend to lower the standard of religion. We must admit that neither science nor religion is the business of a magician.

In every religion there are essential things, and around them grow many things which have no direct bearing on religion. We know there are cheats and charlatans in the field of so-called religion. At the same time we should admit that there are dishonest persons in every walk of life, but counterfeit coins only indicate that there are genuine ones. No true prophet asks us to take anything granted merely because he believes to be true. The genuine prophets say : "Experiment yourself and you are sure to reach the same conclusion." The process is the same with science, but the only difference is that in science we can see, while in religion we have to feel and realize.

Thus we see that the goal of science is material achievement; that of religion is realization. Man cannot live by body alone. When he is tired of materialism, he feels some hidden want of esoteric spiritualism. And in this way science and religion maintain their parallel courses for seeking light from the external and internal world. And so James Sturat Mill said, "If there is no God, God should be created by man."

Religion takes us to lofty levels of deep realization.As the greatest scientist of all times—Albert Einstein—has synthesized in his deep ulterance : 'My realigion consists of a humble admiration of the illimitable superior spirit—slight details of whose creation we are able to perceive with our frail and feeble minds. That deeply emotional conviction of the presence of a superior spirit, which is revealed in the incomprehensible universe, forms my idea of God.'

23. SCIENCE AND SUPERSTITIONS

Introduction : What is science and what is superstition?

Evils of superstition : deprives a man of his power of reasoning—crooked offspring of ignorance—superstition still prevailing even after bold attempts of some scientists.

Some instances of superstition : eclipse of the sun—sneezing, ticking of a lizard, crying of an owl, moaning of a dog, a black cat at night, odd number of thirteen, etc.—epidemic of cholera or pox as the blessing of the goddess Shitala—wearing rings of special stones, etc.

Science as the cure : superstition a disease and science, the remedy—not only bookish scientific knowledge, but the scientific outlook is needed

●

We know man is, on the whole, a rational being. And science is an instrument by which man can find truth by experiments and the power of reasoning. With our advancement of civilization, people are making their way through the darkness of ignorance with the help of the searchlight of science. On the other hand, superstition is a blind faith of an individual. It may, of course, spread into a society or a nation.

Superstition is perhaps the greatest enemy of all kinds of progress. It deprives a man of his power of reasoning and resists any new scientific ideas as much as it can. In fact, there is an inherent contradiction between science and superstition. Superstition is the sworn enemy of science. Scientific ideas gain potency only in proportion to its success in the battle against superstition. Superstition is the crooked offspring of ignorance. And so it tries to honour ignorance as sacred and permanent without any rhyme and reason. So Bruno, Galileo and Copernicus stood against superstition for promoting science even at the cost of their lives. But superstition has not totally lost its force till today.

There are so many superstitions in our society. An eclipse of the sun is inauspicious to some superstitious people. If someone sneezes, or calls us from behind at the time of starting, we lose our self-confidence. Even if a house-lizard ticks, it is regarded by many as ominous for a journey! The cry of an owl, the moaning of a dog or a black cat at night may frighten a man as a sign of bad luck. We see that the ignorant village people treat the epidemic of cholera or pox as the blessing of the goddess Shitala. The so-called civilized and elite people also have some superstitions such as their notion about the odd number of thirteen. Even some teachers of science wear rings with special stones or metals to pacify the planets supposed to be angry with them.

The ignorance and weakness of character is, as a whole, the cause, and superstition is the effect. And, if we really mean to eradicate an evil effect, we must direct our attack against the cause from which it springs. It we treat superstition as a disease, science should be regarded as the right medicine to cure it. This is precisely what science does in the relentless battle against superstition. Of course, here science means not only the bookish knowledge of science, but the scientific spirit in its truest sense. And if we really want to be free from superstition, this scientifice spirit must go deep into our social system and change our attitude from within.

24. SCIENCE AND WAR
OR
WAR AND PEACE

Introduction : Modern war depends much on science—Science is often thought to be responsible for war

Wars fought even before the development of science : There were wars even before science was much developed—people mad for power in all ages

Science changes the technique of war : now a push-button affair instead of battlefields—atom bombs—missiles—Star War—preventive measure by signing CTBT

Mutual distrust : The Super Powers agreed to destroy some weapons, still racing to pile up stronger and deadlier weapons

Science prevents war also : Each country is afraid of attacking other countries lest it should spark a World War and be destroyed itself

War and peace : a period of war is a period of chaos and confusion—on the other hand development of civilization embracing arts and science owes its growth and nourishment to peace—creative gifts of peace far more lasting than the gifts of war—a better world to our future generations

Conclusion : responsibility of science not for war only, but for peace too

●

War in modern times is completely different from the local fights of the earlier times. Now it is highly technical operation and it depends much on science. The art of war has now become the science of warfare. Almost all the modern inventions of science are now being used in modern war. Now war is nothing but 'organised butchery of boys'. And so science is often thought to be responsible for war.

There were wars even before science was much developed. Wars are fought because there are some people who are mad for power, and such people exist in all ages.

War is now a push-button affair, especially in the nuclear war, instead of the fight in battlefields. Ballistic missiles are thrown from a long distance. The atom bombs that destroyed Hiroshima and Nagasaki are nothing compared with those that are stock-piled by the Super Powers of the world today. Even India and Pakistan have recently acquired nuclear power. The latest addition in warfare is 'Star War' which can abolish life from this planet. Even biological weapons of germs and poisonous gas (WMD) are being made to annihilate the people of an enemy country by slow poisoning. It is seen that superiority in armaments is the deciding factor in a modern war. Each side now makes it a point to prevent the manufacture of these weapons by the other side. So the USA is putting pressure on India after the nuclear test explosion at Pokhran for signing the CTBT.

Mutual distrust is so intense that though the Super Powers have agreed to destroy some weapons, they are still racing against each other to pile up stronger and deadlier weapons. This has placed us on the threshold of a third World War. It is high time to remember that force is not a final solution for man's problems. Force on its own is nothing. Yet the common people look on it with shuddering helplessness.

However, from another point we can see that the development of science prevents war also. Each country is now afraid of attacking other countries lest it should spark a World War and be destroyed itself.

Now it is the time to cry not for war, but for peace. We should realise that a period of war is a period of chaos and confusion. The peace-loving people of the world are horrified to see the frenzied activities of the war-mongers who derive devilish delight by killing countless innocent men, women and children. The chief function of war is to destroy all the symbols of civilization, to batter down and burn cities and towns to multiply the number of widows and orphans, to turn the fruitful fields, the flora and fauna into deserts. So widespread is the destruction that in some cases nothing is left of a country except scorched earth. On the other hand, development of civilization embracing arts and science depends on peaceful condition of a country. Architecture, sculpture, painting, music, philosophy, literature, agriculture and even trade and industry owe their birth, growth and nourishment to peace. These creative gifts of peace are far more lasting than the gifts of war. Hence we want peace, not war; we want amity, not enmity; we want fine arts, not fire-arms; we want flowering fields, not the desert of destruction so that we can gift a better world to our future generations.

There are many who speak as though science is responsible for war. But science cannot be blamed for this dreadful situation. It is the warmongers who are responsible for this. We can use fire for cooking our food or burning others' houses! It is not the fault of fire, but of its users. It is an irony of fate that while 60% of the world's population live below the poverty line and millions die for want of food, different governments spend billions of dollars in military budget only. Can we not buy peace and save the mankind with the huge amount we spend for the preparation of war? In such a context we should melt swords, the symbol of war into ploughshares, and turn 'Science for War' into 'Science for Peace', as the supreme value of human life, human blood and human dignity should not be forgotten in any way.

25. STUDENTS AND POLITICS

Introduction : need of political awareness in a democracy

Students' primary duty : a student's primary duty is to study—prepare himself for his future life—active involvement in politics may curtail time to study and ruin a student's carreer

Present position of politics : a dirty game full of passion, ill-feeling and excitement—students should be aware of professional politicians—politicians should not be allowed to exploit student power—however important the political issues may be, politicians must be kept off the campus of the institutions

Students' participation in the struggle for freedom : active involvement justified in pre-independence period—the role of the students in free India is different

Conclusion : knowledge of socio-political condition and economic programmes of the country and debates, discussions, seminars are necessary.

●

There is no doubt about the need of political awareness of students in a democratic country. But the question arises whether they should have active participation in it or not. And in this point we see that though the spheres of students and politicians are different, there are some persons who are in favour of students' participation in politics and there are some others who are against it.

The primary duty of a student is to study and thereby to acquire knowledge and prepare himself for his future life. If a student becomes actively involved in politics and becomes a member of a political party, he is sure to devote less time to study and his future career may be ruined. The present indiscipline and unrest among students is largely due to their active participation in politics.

In fact, active politics is a dirty game full of passion, ill-feeling and excitement nowadays. Once the students are actively involved in politics, they tend to be a plaything in the hand of unscrupulous politicians who exploit them for their own narrow ends. Such politicians appeal to the emotional youths because they are easily available to lengthen the size of the processions, to muster strong in the meeting ground, to utter all sorts of high-sounding catch-words and so on. Students should be aware of such professional politicians. Over-active politicians should not be allowed to exploit student power. However important the political issues may be, politicians must be kept off the campus of the institutions.

When India was not free, students' participation in the struggle for freedom was justified. But in free India, the role of the students should be different. Partisan politics generates more heat than light and brings in narrowness. So we should think deeply over the whole issue from an unbiased point of view.

Students, however, should not remain ignorant of politics. They should know how the governments of different countries function and how their own country is governed. They should have knowledge of the socio-political condition of the country. They should also study the political and economic programmes of the different political parties of the country and try to form their own opinion of them by arranging debates, discussions, seminars, etc. Thus they should take notice of the cross-currents of politics of their own country and the trend of world events. But, by no means, they should become the pawns on the political chess-board.

26. GOOD MANNERS

Introduction : what it means—includes politeness, humility, kind words and courtesy

Good manners make a man civilised : turns a two-legged animal to be a civilised man— helps to win friends and foes — the small coins of virtue — should be nurtured from childhood

How to reflect good manners? : costs nothing but adds value to life—to say 'Sorry', 'Please', 'Thank You', etc.—soft word and sweet voice—good sense and good feeling—show due respect to others' feeling and opinions—show kindness to ladies, children, the old, weak and disabled persons

Some examples : to offer a seat to an old or a weak man in a train or bus—not to smoke in a crowded bus or train—not to throw litter here and there—to stand in a queue before a booking counter—cover one's mouth while coughing—not to go on talking without listening to others—keeping the surroundings clean—not to damage any public property

Conclusion : brings happiness and success—builds character

●

Manner is habitual conduct. It is good when it tends to be positive in relation to fellow human beings. It is bad when it hurt others. Everybody has his/her own style of conduct in his/her family and society at large. A man with good manners is liked and admired by all. Such a man does not want to hurt anyone by his behaviour. Good manners include politeness, humility, kind words and courtesy. It is like a magic-stone that can turn a raw material into gold. And so Montague said : "Good manners cost nothing, but buy everything."

Man without good manners is like a savage animal. Only good manners can turn such a two-legged animal to be a man. A costly dress cannot make a man civilised, but good manners can do it. Good manners go a long way in making a man cultured in various aspect and achieve a good result. It helps him not only to obtain friends but also to win foes. It is an influential power in society. It helps him to possess a pleasing personality. It is rightly said : "Good manners are the small coins of virtue." It is this quality that should be nurtured from the very childhood.

It is truly said—good manners can do a miracle. It costs nothing but adds value to life. Politeness and courtesy are the key word to good manners. The polite words like 'Sorry', 'Please' and 'Thank You' can create a pleasant impression on others around us. Words spoken at the right time in a soft and sweet voice are bound to work wonders. Good manners are the blossom of good sense and good feeling. One should show due respect for the feeling and opinion of others. Good manners consist in showing kindness to ladies, children, the old, the weak and disabled persons. We should always offer help to them, as and when necessary.

It is a common scene that a young man is seated and an old or a weak person is standing before him in a train or a bus. Good manners demand that we should offer them our seats spontaneously. We should not smoke in a crowded bus or train. We should not throw banana skin or any litter on the road or on the railway platform. It may cause someone to slip and suffer a fall. We should always stand in a queue before the booking counter and do not elbow others to get through it, but wait patiently for our turn. While coughing we must cover our mouth with a handkerchief. We must not go on talking to others without listening to what they have to say. We should keep our surroundings clean and do not damage any public property under any pretext.

A good-mannered person is free from sternness, harshness and violence. He/She is amiable, soft and moderate. Such a person is a good neighbour and a reliable friend. He/She is always the centre of attraction. Thus we see that good manners bring happiness and success in one's life. They are the basis of building one's character. So we must acquire good manners and a pleasing personality.

27. LIFE IS WORK/LIFE IS DUTY
OR
LIFE IS AN ACTION, NOT CONTEMPLATION

Introduction : duty and contemplation defined

Men and lower animals : Men live to work, while lower animals work to live—both body and mind get rust without work

Duties of a man : duties to one's family, neighbours and friends—duties to his country, to people in distress and duty to mankind

Examples of great men of action : men in different fields of work—statesmen like Mahatma Gandhi, George Washington, Abraham Lincoln, Nelson Mandela, Martin Luther King etc.—preachers and social workers like Swami Vivekananda, Mother Teresa, etc.—scientists like Newton, Einstein, J. C. Bose, A . P. J. Abdul Kalam etc.—writers like Shakespeare, Milton, Rabindranath Tagore, etc.—in business John D, Rockfeller, Bill Gates, etc.

Conclusion : harmonious blend of action and contemplation —noble thoughts and deeds make the world richer and happier.

●

Duty is an action due from us to ourselves, our family, our neighbours, fellow-men and the whole human race. Contemplation is a mental exercise. It may be meditative or it may be just brooding over the past events, or just dreaming for fulfilment of one's desires. The first kind of contemplation is very useful as it helps a man to recover his confidence and recharge the battery of his mind. But the second and third type of contemplation is a curse as it leads a man to lose all initiative and enthusiasm for living an idle life, not an ideal life.

Man is the noblest of all living beings and his superiority is due to his manifold activities. In fact, human beings live to work, while lower animals work to live. Animals are found to work for the satisfaction of their physical needs, and they cease to exert themselves as soon as they get sufficient food for immediate consumption. But man does not cease to work when his momentary wants have been satisfied. He works for the future. Again, man must work to feed his mind and spirit. Otherwise, if a man remains idle, both his body and mind get rusted without work.

Duty starts from childhood in a loose and indirect manner. But when a man reaches his adulthood, his duties become more exacting and burdensome. Besides his duties to his family, neighbours and friends, he will be called upon to undertake higher duties — duty to his country, duty to people in distress and duty to mankind. Hence, every station in life has duties appropriate to it. The performance of all these duties requires the constant cultivation of all the faculties of man. Thus he can build his character strong enough not to yield to any temptation. Such a man is admired by all for his activities during his life-time, and after his death, he continues to live in the minds of men. And so the proverb goes—"Man lives in deeds, not in age."

If we study the lives of great men, we shall find that they were all inspired with a lofty sense of duty in life. They were stalwarts in different fields of work. We can site examples of the discoverers and noble travellers like Columbus, Fa-Hien, Hiu-en-Tsang, Edmund Hillary, Tenzing, etc., the statesmen like Mahatma Gandhi, George Washington, Abraham Lincoln, Nelson Mandela, Martin Luther King, etc., preachers and social workers like Swami Vivekananda, Mother Teresa, etc., scientists like Newton, Einstein, J. C. Bose, Acharya Prafullachadra Roy, Satyen Bose etc., writers like Shakespeare, Milton, Rabindranath Tagore, etc., and in business Jameshedji Tata, John D. Rockfeller, Bill Gates, etc. They rose to the occasion, fought the challenge of life heroically, and succeeded in their objectives. These great men learnt the secret of success that consists in action, not in idle contemplation.

Finally we can say—what we need in our life is a harmonious blend of action and contemplation. We must remember that noble thoughts and deeds ultimately make the world richer and happier.

28. LEISURE—ITS USES AND ABUSES

Introduction : What it means

Need for leisure : constant work brings boredom and fatigue—leisure gives us rest—releases from the monotony of toil—refreshes tired nerves, and provides vigour and energy

Products of leisure and action combined : art, science, philosophy and culture

Ways of spending leisure : taking some hobbies—going out to countryside or some places of interest—enjoying solitary walks—indoor or outdoor games—reading favourite books, magazines, etc.—useful but light social works

Abuse of leisure : loitering, gossiping, back-biting, eve-teasing—drinking, gambling, playing cards, etc.

Conclusion : leisure to forget cares and worries—introspection of an individual

●

Leisure means freedom from occupation in the free time at one's disposal. In fact, it is the time when we are our own master and at liberty to pass our time in the manner we choose. As civilisation has developed, we have become busier and leisure is being progressively decreased. But we should keep in mind the proverb— "All work and no play makes Jack a dull boy."

Constant work brings boredom and fatigue to a man and surely chokes the mainspring of his vitality. And for that we need leisure to provide rest for our muscles and limbs. It refreshes our tired nerves and makes us fit for our work with a new vigour and energy. It releases us from the monotony of toil and worries of duty and makes our mind afresh. As a machine needs rest and oiling, so it is for a human body. Without leisure human life would have been a dull affair. Aristotle, the great philosopher, said that leisure is an essential condition of happiness.

Leisure has been rightly described as the mother of art, science, philosophy and culture, as leisure provides us with time for deep thought and meditation. And we get the products of arts and science when these thoughts of leisure are transformed into action.

Of course, leisure should be properly used. It should not be wasted away in idleness as it is rightly said, "An idle brain is a devil's workshop." There are various ways of spending one's leisure. During leisure one should pursue some hobbies according to one's trend of mind. Some go out to the countryside or some places of interest and feed their senses with charming sights and sounds of nature. Some others enjoy solitary walks, indoor or outdoor games, and pleasant talks with friends and families. Book-lovers can turn over the pages of some favourite books, magazines, etc. We may undertake some useful but light social works too. In short, it is necessary for all of us to spend our leisure with something non-essential in which our mind may have rest and relaxation instead of multiplying hours of work to earn a surplus income.

However, we see that leisure is often abused. Many men spend it in loitering or in idle gossiping over trifle matters. There are many 'idlers' who sit on outer verandahs of houses or 'rocks'—or stand at street-corners or parks and pass time by backbiting others, or passing objectionable remarks on the passers-by. Sometimes the young boys find pleasure in eve-teasing. Some others waste their leisure by drinking, gambling, playing cards, etc.

At any rate leisure should not be wasted in restless pursuit of any unworthy object. Actually we require leisure as it helps us to forget for a time the cares and worries of life and to stand and stare at the intervals of work. William Davies rightly says in his poem 'Leisure" —

"What is this life, if full of care
We have no time to stand and stare?"

29. HUMOUR—THE SPICE OF LIFE

Introduction : the original meaning of 'humour' and its later development—capability to laugh and make other laugh—importance in our day-to-day relationship—the spice of life

Good humour, a valuable defence : an aid against worries—helps to come out of odd situations—not to hurt others

A healthy attitude to life : useful to maintain mental balance—derives happiness from little things of life—develops self-awareness

Sense of humour, a characteristic of great men : some examples in different fields of life

Conclusion : kings and official fools—Presidents, Prime Ministers, etc. in the garb of cartoons—laughing clubs—target of our humour also can mend their behaviour

●

The word 'humour' originally meant a fluid. The mediaeval doctors believed that there were four prominent fluids or humours in the body—blood, phlegm, choler and melancholy; and that a man's physical and mental characteristics were determined by the ratio of those properties. This doctrine has now been abandoned, but 'humour' has remained in the sense of good temperament or state of mind. It is the power to appreciate wit and fun and it gives us the ability to laugh and make others laugh. It plays an important role in our daily routine of life and relationship. In fact, it is the spice of life.

Good humour is also a valuable defence in fighting against worries and in battles of life. It energises us not to get upset in the face of every misfortune, and helps us to come out of odd situations. But a joke is never humorous if it is done to hurt others. On the other hand, a good-humoured person is one who is not easily provoked or irritated, takes things in a genial and friendly spirit and gets a pleasant companion.

It is a healthy attitude to life. It is also a good habit and may be cultivated throughout one's life. Life is neither too good nor too bad. It is what you make of it. If you develop an attitude of looking at the dark side of life only, you cannot enjoy your life. On the other hand, if you have some sense of humour, you will find something consoling or even amusing in many unhappy situations. Humour is thus the defining characteristic between the pessimist and the optimist. It is useful to maintain mental balance and adds spice to otherwise stale parties in many occasions. And people with a strong sense of humour become very popular and their presence in any gathering is highly appreciated. In this way humour helps people to derive happiness from little things of life and develops self-awareness.

We can see the sense of humour as a characteristic of great men too. Albert Einstein, Rabindranath Tagore and Swami Vivekananda, among the greatest men of recent times, were gifted with great wit and humour. They had the ability even to laugh at themselves. The literary figures like Shakespeare, Shaw, Dickens and Lamb have depicted life in varied colours, and humour shines there like a flash of lightning. It not only attracts a large number of readers, but also ensures them a high place among the all-time greats in the field of literature.

So, instead of getting angry when something goes wrong, we should try to look for the humour in odd situations. It eases tensions and can make even the worst of situations tolerable. In earlier times there were official buffoons—jesters— to amuse the kings. Now the Presidents and Prime Ministers who have taken the place of kings have no such scope of amusement. But they too, are in the garb of amusing cartoons, exciting our laughter. There are laughing clubs for the public too. But they contain very little humour. Rather they supply some exercise of lungs to get the people satisfied to fill their quota of laughter for the day. Humour acts in a greater way, and through it we can learn to relax and look at the flaw of life in amusing attitude. Even the targets of laughter can also mend their behaviour in a balanced manner.

30. MODERN TIMES AND ADVERTISEMENT

Introduction : effective means of promoting one's own business or requirements —means to survive through keen competition—products come to public notice

Medium of advertisement : Radio, TV, newspapers—hoardings, glow-sign boards, placards, stickers, handbills, humorous cartoons, etc.

Art and objects of advertisement : great art is to know how to catch the eye and the pocket of the buyers—repetitive for a lasting impression—cars, machines, houses or flats, books, etc. come under advertisement

Usefulness : what we lose in one hand, gain on the roundabouts—ensures that a product will maintain its quality—a competition offering the customers a wider choice

Abuses : It assaults not only our eyes, but also our pockets—the trap of advertisement is sometimes a threat to man's well-being

Conclusion : unavoidable in the days of globalistion and market economy—some advertisements are amusing, witty and interesting, some others too fanciful or lavish—the trend of market becomes the ultimate regulator

●

We are living in an age of advertisement. Day-by-day its domination is increasing in every walk of life. It is a most effective means of promoting one's own business or requirements. It is also the useful means to survive through keen competition with rival companies. Through advertisement all sorts of products come to public notice and impress their presence in the market. We cannot but be influenced by the advertisements in modern times.

Next to the electronic media such as Radio or TV, the widely circulated medium of advertisement is the newspaper. Besides, there are hoardings, glow-sign boards, placards, stickers, handbills, humorous cartoons, etc. to catch the customers.

The great art of advertisement is to know how to catch the eye and the pocket of the buyers. For lasting impression, advertisement should be repetitive— because, by constant hammering one can attract the attention of the public. In order to promote the purpose of an organisation or to boost sales of some commodities — cars, machines, houses or flats or even newly published books, the producer or the publisher takes the help of advertisement. One may take help of advertisement for getting one's personal requirement too. Thousands of experts are engaged in finding out novel methods to arrest the attention of the prospective consumers. Very often the approach is psychological rather than a plain claim of superiority.

In our country 1.6% of the national income is spent on advertising, and this advertising actually raises the cost of products. When a housewife buys a packet of a reputed brand of detergent powder, about 5% of what she pays goes to the advertiser as the cost of advertising the name. Businessmen invest a lot of money on advertisement because they know it pays in return. However, we see that some of the advertisements give truthful account of their products; others give misleading information. Sometimes the consumers are benefited, and sometimes they are deceived by them. But there are some points to be said in its favour. Though some things cost more because of advertising, other related things cost less. Newspapers, commercial radio and TV — all carry advertisements and the money received from the advertisers helps to lower the sale price of these media items. And in this way what we lose on the swings, we gain on the roundabouts. Apart from this, advertising, to some extent, ensures that a product will maintain its quality. It also gives rise to a competition among manufacturers, which benefits the customers by offering him a wider choice. Above all, the best advertiser is he who can promote the freeze in the land of Eskimos.

But advertisements have their abuses too. Critics point out that the overdose of advertising assaults not only our eyes but also our pockets. The trap of advertisement is sometimes a threat to man's well-being when it tries to promote the sale of things that we do not really need; or even more, when it tempts people to buy and consume things that may reduce their savings, heath and happiness.

In the days of globalisation and market economy, the investment in the field of advertisement has reached its peak. Buyers ought to know the real worth of the consumer goods or medicines or books being produced and put up for sale. Advertisement helps them in that direction, and in that sense some advertisements amuse us in a pleasant way, or strike us as witty and interesting, but most of them are either too fanciful or inducive to lavishness. We all feel the overdose of advertisement, but are helpless when the trend of market becomes the ultimate regulator.

31. HUMAN RIGHTS

Introduction : What it is

Origin and development : beginning of an institutionalised social order in civil and religious rights, then in economic and political rights—bring the minorities and the unprivileged under special protection

Victims in the State and International level : the poor and the unprivileged—opponents of the government suppressed by imposing emergency—Mrs. Suu Kyi in Mayanamar, Miss Taslima Nasrin from Dhaka, etc.

International observation : the estimate of Amnesty International—international public opinion

What about terrorists ? : Should the terrorists be allowed to claim human rights?

Constitution and activities of Human Rights Commission : Most of the countries have formed Human Rights Commission recommending many proposals including the condition of the prison and safeguard of the women-folk

Conclusion : Human Rights Commission must have adequate power to fit the situation

●

Human rights are some basic rights as human beings in a civilised society. These are rights of life and property, of food and clothes, of freedom of movement and expression of opinion. As a whole, it should be honoured in every civilised society and it is the most talked-about subject today in the civilised world.

Its origin can be traced in the beginning of an institutionalised social order. It has travelled a long path since then. Now it covers new areas constantly. At first it was confined to civil and religious rights of the individual. Then it has been extended to economic and political rights. These include the rights of the minorities and the unprivileged under special protection.

In fact, human society all over the world is today broadly divided into two groups — the rich and the poor, the 'haves' and the 'have-nots', the privileged class enjoying all good things of life and the helpless unprivileged who remain as they were. To make things worse, the opponents of the government of some States also are deprived of legitimate human rights. This intolerance often leads to imprisonment of the protester with or without trial in law-courts. Third-degree methods of inhuman torture are applied on the political prisoners in some countries by imposing emergency. In some countries military heads have captured power directly or with the help of some puppets. The destiny of the common people is trodden under the steamroller of the autocrats, and all these do not always come to light. Mrs. Suu Kyi who won the last general election in Mayanamar and later on won the Nobel Peace Prize was till the other day under house-arrest. Miss Taslima Nasrin cannot return to her hometown Dhaka till now, as the fundamentalists of Bangladesh give constant threats to kill her.

In the estimate of Amnesty International it is exposed that a large number of prisoners are detained without trial in jails in some countries including India. The only silver lining is that international public opinion is snowballing to protect the human rights all over the world. Now the study of human rights is becoming the great concern for both national and international lawyers, diplomates, statesmen, reformers, activists, policy-makers and citizens of different countries.

However, the question has been recently raised whether the militants and well-armed terrorists who seek to destabilise the States, sometimes aided by foreign countries, should also be allowed to come under the purview of the sacred code of human rights. Some say that terrorism flourishes on frustration on economic and political grounds. So, the best way to solve the problems is to offer an open call to the so-called terrorists and talk and settle the knotty issues in a cordial spirit.

At present the constitutions of most of the countries which believe in the rules of law have incorporated the provisions of basic human rights. In India there has been set up an Apex Body of Human Rights and its State branches have also been organised. Their activities have been welcomed by the weaker sections of the society. They are recommending many proposals including the condition of the prison and safeguard of the women-folk.

But the State governments as well as the Central government tend to ignore their recommendations where their interests clash. It proves that Human Rights Commission must have adequate power to fit the situation. It is a matter of shame and disgrace that as yet there is no such national or international authority with mandatory powers to prevent those who indulge in the nefarious game of violating human rights.

32. OLYMPIC 2012

Hints : opening ceremony of sporting extravaganza on July 27 at the Olympic Park Stadium at Stratford in London—a grand sight of badminton, football and women's volleyball on July 29—gymnastic on July 30—swimming on July 31—Long jump, 10,000 m final and women's 100 m final on August 4—different events including sailing on August 5—swimming, women's boxing, and boxing including old men's event on August 6—the end of 200 m dash on August 9—football final, 5,000 m race, hockey final, boxing on August 11—wrestling, basket ball final and closing caremony on August 12.

●

The opening ceremony of Olympic sporting extravaganza started at the Olympic Park Stadium at Stratford in London on July 27. The first interesting event was badminton on July 29. What a grand sight it was, the panoramic arch of Wembly stadium with the Olympic symbol set against a deep purple backdrop! People of all ages sporting their country colours were arriving at the stadium for football matches too. And one of the most attractive events was women's beach volleyball.

On July 30 the most visible Olympic fans across the city were British and American, though there were many Europeans and Asians as well. The whole arena was deep purple-pink and the gymnastic floor was immaculate. In the team event Japan was ranking second, after China. The Great Britain team was pushed to bronze. They were greeted by Prince William in the stands as this was the first Olympic medal in gymnastics for GB in a 100 years!

On July 31 the greatest Olympian of all time, American swimmer Michael Phelps, won gold for his team in the 4 × 200 m freestyle relay and silver in the individual 200 m butterfly. On August 4 came the event of long jump. Team GB's Greg Rutherford won the event soaring to 8.31 m. The 10,000 m final was won by Mo Farah. During the women's 100 m final, the crowd went mad yelling with joy as Jamaican Shellay-Ann Fraser-Pryce aced the race in 10.75 seconds.

On August 5 in the evening at Wimbledon, Andy Murray took sweet revenge beating Roder Frederer in straight sets. And on the sea-side in Weymouth, Ben Ainslle became the greatest British Olympian in sailing by getting his fourth gold in four consecutive games.

On August 6 US swimmer Missy Franklin won four golds and the 16-year-old Chinese swimmer Ye Shiwen brought the aquatic centre alive by breaking the world record in the 400 m individual event. Ethiopian runner Tirunesh Dibaba bagged her third Olympic gold medal. And for us, there was boxer Mary Kom who showed grit and won bronze. The Olympic games did not ignore older enthusiastics either. Hiroshi Hoketsu, a 71-year-old Japanese showjumper was the oldest participant. The evening of August 9 was lit up yet again at the end of the 200 m dash .

On August 11 the football final game was full of Brazilian skills, but they were unable to score except in the closing moments. The 2-1 score in favour of Mexico lit the stadium with green. Germans won the hockey final with a narrow margin of 2-1 against the Dutch. British boxers excelled in the ring, and in wrestling, our Yogeshwar Dutt won bronze in the 60 kg freestyle category. On August 12 our Sushil Kumar won silver in 66 kg wrestling.

India feels frustration of a great nation with such small returns. A country of 1.2 billion people managed just 2 silvers and 4 bronze medals. Even Grenada (with a population of only 1,10,000) bagged a gold. Can we not show our glory in a more befitting manner in the Olympics?

33. U 19 WORLD CUP CRICKET 2012

&

TEST MATCH VICTORY IN HYDERABAD

Hints : The victory of India in U 19 World Cup Cricket in Australia in 2012 after 2000 in Sri Lanka and 2008 in Malaysia—Captain Unmukt Chand unbeaten 111—hit seven fours and six sixes—wicketkeeper Smit Patel scored 62 to a winning 227 for four—Sandeep Sharm's 4 for 54 helped restrict Australia to 225 for eight—Rabikant's one for 41 to end the tournment—in Hyderabad the pair of Aswin and Pragyan took 18 of 20 wickets in the innings—Captain Dhoni's team hitting 438 against New Zealand's 159 + 164—Aswin Man of the Match

●

This time the victory under the captaincy of Unmukt Chand in Australia gave India their third World Cup title, after Md Kaif and Virat Kohli had lifted the trophies in 2000 in Sri Lanka and 2008 in Malaysia. Captain Unmukt Chand's unbeaten 111 lifted India to victory in the U 19 World Cup Cricket on Sunday (26 August 2012). It is a day of days! Chand hit seven fours and six sixes while the wicketkeeper Smit Patel secured a composed 62, as the duo lifted India to a winning 227 for four. The opening bowler Sandeep Sharma's 4 for 54 had helped restrict Australia to 225 for eight. The Calcutta boy Ravikant ('Bittu') Singh, a fast-medium bowler, chipped in with one for 41 to end the tournament.

In Hyderbad India won the test match against New Zealand on the same day. The pair of Aswin and Pragyan took 18 of 20 wickets in the first and second innings. Captain Dhoni's team hit 438 in first innings against New Zealand's 159 + 164 in two innings. Aswin was declared Man of the Match without any debate. Thus we see the seniors cannot be left behind when the colts have done us proud with an inspirational World Cup triumph. If Unmukt Chand's team showed grit and dedication at Tony Ireland Stadium in Townsville on Sunday, Mahendra Singh Dhoni's men proved equally adept to beat New Zealand, 24 minutes after tea, on the penultimate day of the first match in Hyderabad.

PARAGRAPHS ON PROVERBS

1. ALL THAT GLITTERS IS NOT GOLD

Gold is a shining metal. It is a precious thing and its glitter dazzles our eyes. It is precious for its intrinsic worth. There are other things which, though they glitter like gold, are by no means as precious as gold, as they have no such intrinsic value. A gilt ornament has the same lustre of gold. But it is not considered so valuable, because after a test it is found lacking in its intrinsic virtue. So the proverb signifies that nothing should be judged merely by appearances, as appearances may be deceptive. We should be aware of the world which is full of snares. Vice frequently puts on the garb for virtue, and hypocrisy passes for sincerity. Things are not always what they seem. However, the proverb does not at all suggest that we should always be sceptical. It only emphasises the importance of being careful while reposing trust in others.

2. A LITTLE LEARNING IS A DANGEROUS THING

The real significance of this proverb seems to be that man should always try to make an exact estimate of his own worth. He ought not to pose as a learned man, if he is not really so. It he wants to show that he has the worth and capacities of a really learned man and act likewise, he becomes a danger to society. In fact, learning is always good and it is not little learning that creates our misfortune. But the conceit in a foolish man creates the troubles. Let us take a concrete example. Suppose, a man is seriously injured in an accident. It is good to have a little knowledge to start the first-aid. But thereafter he should be taken to a hospital for proper treatment. It would be dangerous to presume that we know much and treat the patient ourselves. Quacks in all the fields may offer some timely help, but it poses to be dangerous when they cross their limit. And so, in order to avoid dangers of a little knowledge, we should be clear about how much we know and make a positive effort to know more.

3. A ROLLING STONE GATHERS NO MOSS

It is a matter of common observation that a piece of stone lying in a marshy place for a long time gets covered with moss. But if it keeps rolling with the current, it gathers no moss. The proverb figuratively means that a man who does not settle down to a fixed profession or occupation never gets success. A plant removed from place to place can never thrive well. It is often found that the traveller who follows his course with determination will sooner reach the goal than one who always changes direction. There is none so unlucky as the man who always changes his mind. He has no fixed principle of purpose. Like a weathercock he turns with the wind. As a result he will never attain success and become the victim of disappointment and discontent. However, a modern writer says in the opposite way—a rolling stone gathers moss. In his opinion, a person who is not idly settled in one place, but seeks fortune in different fields may get some moss or prosperity in this or that place.

4. A BIRD IN HAND IS WORTH TWO IN THE BUSH

This proverb suggests that we should not be too greedy in our day-to-day activities. We should have some contentment with what we have. Legitimate ambition and struggle to rise in life are commendable, while unreasonable greed and craze to get something always lands one into serious trouble. We know the fable of the greedy dog who, having a piece of meat in its own mouth, saw its shadow in the river and jumped from the bridge to snatch it too. As a result, it lost its own piece of meat and its life too. The story of king Midas is also an eye-opener in this context. Not being satisfied with his own treasures, Midas begged the boon of golden touch, and lost his food, his drinking water and even his dearest daughter! Finally, he begged the goddess of wealth to return him to his previous state. In our times, we find the fate of many people who go to foreign countries as unauthorised immigrants to get rich quickly and come back disappointed having lost all their previous possessions. Some of these people even lose their life and honour. So we should be aware of our unreasonable greed and ambition.

5. AN IDLE BRAIN IS THE DEVIL'S WORKSHOP

A man who whiles away his time in idleness is often tempted to do wicked deeds. He has to fight against many passions and resist the temptations that come in his way. It is not an easy task to keep one's evil propensities under control. But we have a friend who helps us considerably. And that friend is work. Work keeps the mind occupied and does not permit it to run wild. But an idle man devotes his energies to pursuits harmful to himself as well as to others. What is worse, he will seek bad company. Of course, it is not wise to be always engaged in work. We know — all work and no play makes Jack a dull boy. And so we should make a bàlance between work and leisure. And that leisure too should be used in some hobbies, etc., not in idle gossip, brooding or breeding mischief.

6. AS YOU SOW, SO YOU SHALL REAP

The proverb is taken from the field of agriculture. A cultivator who has ploughed the land carefully, and has sown good seeds may expect a rich harvest. If he does not till his land properly, or sows bad seeds, or sows untimely, his harvest will be poor. It is the rule of cause and effect. If you want to do harm, it will be harmful, if you want to do good, it may produce a good result. Thus good habits formed in childhood will make a man efficient. Otherwise, the evil habits may doom his career. If a man starts lying or stealing, he will grow up to be a confirmed liar or thief, and may one day find himself in jail. It is, therefore, of the utmost importance that we should be careful how we behave or are trained to behave in our childhood. Impression received in childhood survives and influences the rest of life. If we consider the lives of great men, we find that the seeds of their greatness were sown when they were very young. In fact, our past life shapes our present and future.

7. A STITCH IN TIME SAVES NINE

The proverb means that steps should be taken to get remedy of a defect at its earliest stage. If it is done in time, a lot of trouble may be averted. If a tear in a garment is stitched in time, it will stand wear for a much longer time than it is done when the tear become larger. The proverb is applicable to every sphere of life. We often suffer for not being guarded at the first sign of trouble. An example can be given here. A person feels unwell, but does not mind it. When it gets worse, he calls in a doctor, and then his illness has perhaps taken a serious turn. If he had taken care at the outset, much trouble and expense might have been saved. Our bad habits also become serious in this way. Thus we see that timely action is very important in our life, but very few people realise its significances.

8. CHARITY BEGINS AT HOME

It is a common old saying which holds good in our life. Charity should begin from bottom to top, not from top to bottom. Any act of goodness can have solid foundations only if it spreads from the nearest to the farthest. An act of charity must not be undertaken by retaining starvation at home. Any good act must start from one's environment. Similarly, it is sheer hypocrisy to preach to others what we do not practise ourselves. Everybody shouts that there is corruption and nepotism in the country, but when the same person is placed in a position of authority, he, himself often gets involved in such corruption! Of course, there are some great men who sacrifice their lives for the betterment of the greater society. They do not take care of himself or his kith and kin. They do not limit their activities in any narrow boundary. That is also too big an ideal for a common man. The golden mean for a common man is to take care of his family at first, and then he may extend his good spirit to his neighbours, and so on.

9. COWARDS DIE MANY TIMES BEFORE THEIR DEATH

In Shakerspeare's play *Julius Caesar*, Caesar's wife Calphurnia dreamt an ominous dream and feared for Caesar's life. When she said this to her husband, Caesar consoled her by saying, "Cowards die many times before their death" and "The valiant never taste (of death) but once." Actually it is most strange that people fear death even knowing death is inevitable and nothing can prevent it. Bacon once said, "Men fear death as children fear to go in darkness." However, the courageous are not afraid of death. They fully enjoy every moment of their life. On the contrary, cowards meet death many times in their dream or imagination before they actually die. Their whole life is spent in a cowardly manner in fearful anticipation of death. If we interpret it metaphorically, we can say that a person lives truly if he can live with honour; a life of humiliation is a virtual death. Thus a coward is always dying as he lacks the courage to face the challenges of life boldly. But a brave man meets death only when he actually breaths his last.

10. COURTESY COSTS NOTHING

Courtesy or polite dealing is a desirable quality. While exhibited in our dealings with others, courtesy shows a sensible heart and a genial temperament. Courtesy has its place in all our dealings in social life. Like other attributes, courtesy can be acquired by habit. It is an influential power in society. It helps a man to possess a pleasing personality. It helps him not only to obtain friends, but also to win foes. It is rightly said — courtesy can do a miracle. It costs nothing but adds value to life. It is a common scene that a young man is seated and an old or a weak man is standing before him in a train or a bus. Courtesy demands that we should offer the disabled and the senior citizens our seats spontaneously. In fact, courtesy is the basis of building one's character.

11. EXAMPLE IS BETTER THAN PRECEPT

There are two ways of impressing a thing on others. It may be done either by words or by deeds, rather, by precepts or by examples. By precept we can only instruct a man what to be done and the reason why it should be done. But very often the impression created by our advice lasts only as long as the word rings in his years.

In other words, a precept makes only a temporary impression. Students are taught many good things at home or at school. But in spite of that, only a very few obtain the stimulus to be noble and great in life. It can be better done if some good examples are set before them. Parents who wish their children to be good and noble must themselves set before them such good examples. Otherwise no good result will come out of mere advice. If the parents themselves are not good, and give only some good advice, the children cannot be expected to be good, as they are bound to imitate their parents. If you preach something good, and do not follow it yourself, no one will pay heed to you. On the other hand, if a man lives an ideal life of purity and devotion, you will find many who come into contact with him and try to follow him. And so if the leaders of the society are not honest and steady, most of the followers will soon fall back. Biographies of great men may also serve us some good example for following their footsteps.

12. FAILURES ARE THE PILLARS OF SUCCESS

Failure is a stepping stone to success. It produces in man zeal and zest to overcome an obstacle. Life is a battlefield. We cannot expect that we will always win and face no failure. Once Vivekananda said about human sufferings that he who has not faced any sorrows is a newborn baby. A strong character is formed by facing failures and overcoming them. If there is no failure, man becomes easy-going and self-satisfied. He gives up effort and his life become stagnant. Greatness is attained only by meeting failures. Robert Bruce failed to free his country for several times. But he did not give up hope. He was inspired by a spider in his cave, when he saw that the spider could climb the roof at the seventh attempt. Being energised he tried again and won the battle in the long run. The great scientist Einstein was also an utter failure in his young days, but he made wonders in the field of science later on. Thus we see failures act as the pillars to build the roof of success.

13. FORTUNE FAVOURS THE BRAVE
OR
NONE BUT THE BRAVE DESERVES THE FAIR

Some say the goddess of fortune is blind as she bestows her bounty to whom she likes; and it is often whimsically. But if we analyse the true state of things, we find that she is always impartial. She gives her best gifts to the most deserving, to those who are bold and brave. A cowardly man falters at every step. How can he succeed in any enterprise? He is almost faint with fear. When he had launched upon an enterprise, and failure falls to his lot, he is completely undone. But a bold man knows that every adventure is attended with risks, and he takes the risks with cool courage. He calculates where he may fail and is careful to avoid it. He does not get nervous when he is called upon to show his power to the best advantage. He is always equal to the occasion. Such a man scarcely meets with failures. And when he is doomed to fail, he gets the courage to face it in a sportsman's spirit. He does not lose heart, for he has the strength of mind. In fact, boldness consists in one's confidence and intelligence. Such a person ultimately wins the favour of the goddess of fortune. And so "None but the brave deserves the fair" — is an oft-quoted saying which testifies the truth.

14. FRUITS OF LABOUR ARE SWEETER THAN THE GIFTS OF FORTUNE

The maxim teaches us a great truth. What a man earns by the sweat of his brow gives him a greater degree of satisfaction than what he gets by a stroke of fortune.

It is true that man wishes to have many things in life. Some of them may be bestowed with fortune, but there are many who have to toil hard for getting their bread. And these things acquired by hard toil are much sweeter than those a man gets by accident. There is no derth of men who begin their lives with huge amount of money easily obtained from their ancestors, and find themselves pauper before their death. It is because they have never known the struggle for earning money, and they squander away their wealth on frivolous things. What is easily got is lightly valued and easily lost. This is true of every good thing which man loves on earth. When the good thing is bestowed on us without the least exertion on our part, our enjoyment of it is greatly reduced. A self-made man is certainly more happy and more esteemed than the man who owes his fortune to the mere chance of his birth.

15. HE PRAYETH BEST WHO LOVETH BEST

The poet Coleridge, composed these lines with the vision of a prophet—

He prayeth best who loveth best

All things both great and small :

For the dear God who loveth us,

He made and loveth all.

In these simple lines a whole philosophy of human life is embodied as conceived by Buddha, Christ, Sri Chaitanya and Sri Ramakrishna. God loves all of us; therefore all of us should love one another — that is a simple logical proposition.

But the poet goes further. He says that such love is the best form of prayer. We pray to God in order to please Him, to propitiate Him. But God, who is all-seeing, will not be deceived by the empty words of prayer. He will see into our whole life — our feelings and our activities. We may utter God's name a million times every day; we may bow down five times a day as directed by the Quran; we may visit the church every morning and every evening. But all this will be done in vain if our heart is black with hatred for God's creatures. On the other hand, if we love them, God's heart will soften towards us and His blessings will come down on us. Hence the poet says that love is the best form of prayer.

16. HONESTY IS THE BEST POLICY

It may appear to us at first sight that the adoption of unfair means makes our ways smooth. But if we think of the consequences of a dishonest course, it would become clear that honesty is after all the best policy. Thus a boy, when sitting for an examination, may feel tempted to copy from another boy's paper; but if he is detected, he would be expelled or the authorities may debar him from appearing at any future examination. A man who forges currency notes may think that he has discovered a royal road of getting wealthy at ease. But he feels the consequences when he is caught and sent to jail. No dishonest person can escape punishment all the times. Thus dishonesty may bring a man immediate gain, but in the long run it will lead him to ruin. On the other hand, one can see that honesty carries its own reward sooner or later. If you are honest you need not fear anybody. Besides, an honest man is liked and respected by all, even though he is poor. He enjoys the confidence of all who come in contact with him. Above all, he is satisfied with himself.

17. IF WINTER COMES, CAN SPRING BE FAR BEHIND?

Mutation is the law of Nature. And in keeping with this law of change, the seasons come in and go out in a cyclic order. In winter we feel a cold sensation. Trees shed their leaves, stand out sharply against the sky, and put a bleak look. Fields look desolate. The sky wears a mournful grey veil. But the laws of Nature decree that winter cannot rule eternally. After the cold spell of winter, spring appears and everybody welcomes it. The day is sunny and the refreshing spring wind begins to blow. Flowers bloom and the air gets laden with soothing fragrance. The cyclic pattern of Nature is reflected in life as well. Suffering and misfortune may come into one's life for some time, and envelop one's entire existence with drooping despair. But they must inevitably disappear and give way to hope and happiness as the fog disappears before the sun. If someone is able to show fortitude to face the difficulties, he will overcome it. If he can save his vision from being blurred by the mist or cloud, he can perceive a silver lining behind the dark clouds and hopefully wait for the clouds to vanish from the sky. So it is said — even in darkness light dawns for those who believe.

18. IT IS MORE PROFITABLE TO READ ONE MAN THAN TEN BOOKS

Books carry knowledge. And we should take help of books to acquire more knowledge. Undoubtedly it is profitable to read good books as many as possible. But mere bookish knowledge does not take us very far. If it is put to comparison, we see that practical experience earned from a man is more profitable than the theoretical knowledge from books. Books give us the principles, but the application of these principles is more valuable. Application changes with contexts, but books cannot change the contexts as they may vary as and when necessary. We can read the techniques of driving a car or a motorbike from a book at home but we cannot drive the same without having a training from an expert driver. Human life is like a game of chess. We can read the rules that govern the game from a book. But the knowledge of rules does not make a man an expert player. To become a good player, one must play himself, and learn the subtleties and complexities of the game by playing with a variety of players. Similarly, in order to attain success in life, one should meet as many people as possible. And one should try to realise their strength and weakness, their motives and inspirations and their conduct as a whole.

19. KNOWLEDGE IS POWER

Knowledge is power. But here 'power' does not mean the physical ability. It is the power of mind or intellect that can tame his inner self and the outer world. A primitive man was more powerful physically than a civilised man of today. Even a wild animal such as a tiger or a lion or an elephant is more powerful than man. And there is forceful Nature with thunder, lightning, etc. But man has knowledge to make the forces of Nature to serve him. He has turned the power of lightning to electricity. He has tamed the wild elephants to domestic animals. Even the ferocious tigers and lions fear a man with a gun in hand. Not only in the physical world, man has become more and more powerful with the help of science and philosophy with the progress of civilization. Of course, knowledge is of different kinds and grades. It falls under two broad categories — knowledge of the external world and knowledge of one's own self. The sages of ancient India followed both kinds of knowledge and attained amazing success.

20. LOOK BEFORE YOU LEAP

The proverb means that a man should not undertake a risk without careful consideration. He ought to measure his capacity for it and consider whether it is at all proper for him to do it and what consequences are likely to follow. In fact, life is full of pitfalls. So it is necessary to be cautious and careful in our actions. A small leap carelessly or thoughtlessly taken can lead a person to such an abyss from where he may find it impossible to rise. A minor mistake carelessly committed by a person may land him in a situation that may cause him to repent for the rest of his life. Our life is God's greatest gift to us and so it is not to be recklessly frittered away. However, it is not implied here that we should avoid all risks. Risks are a part of life. They provide us with thrill and add colour to it. What we should do is to take the risk carefully with our eyes and ears wide open. On the contrary, it does not also mean that every thoughtful action will lead us to success and prosperity. Life is too unpredictable to ensure it. Sometimes so-called success may appear as deceptive. So it is our duty to consider the pros and cons of an action and carefully visualise its consequences before committing it.

21. MAKE HAY WHILE THE SUN SHINES

It is a well-known maxim. It means that everything must de done at the proper time. Opportunities should never be allowed to go by. Unless you make your hay in summer, it will be difficult in winter. And figuratively it means that a man should avail himself of his opportunities actively and industriously without losing any time. The past and the future are beyond our control and what we can do our best is at the present moment. It is also applicable for a student. If you are a student, study while there is time; for once the examination is over, you can only break your head against your books in vain. It is said that opportunity knocks at the door only but once. So be prepared for its knock and take it in time. Success and happiness do not thrust themselves automatically on anyone. A man himself must win success by doing his duties in time, and by utilising his opportunities. A little courage and perseverance put forth at the proper time are sure to bring their own reward.

22. MAN IS THE MAKER OF HIS DESTINY
OR
EVERY MAN IS THE ARCHITECT OF HIS OWN FORTUNE

It is an old controversy whether man is stronger than his destiny. Some people believe that a man can achieve success if his destiny permits. Others think that man himself carves out his destiny. There is an element of truth in both the beliefs. There are the factors in heredity and environment—how one is born and brought up. Yet it is the fact that we can make our life happy or the reverse by our own activities. A man has in him all those fundamental qualities which are required for achieving greatness, and it depends on him whether he will develop them or not. God is never partial in distributing gifts among men. It is sometimes seen that we fail to attain success in spite of strenuous and repeated efforts. But in most cases, a close scrutiny will reveal that we have committed some mistakes. There may be a few exceptions. But the general rule is in favour of iron will and strong determination. Those who fail in everything owing to their own negligence and idleness blame their fate.

23. NECESSITY IS THE MOTHER OF INVENTION

Wants impel a man to action and invention to get rid of the wants. This may be of various degrees. It may be the invention of a needle or radio transmission. A primitive man invented fire to satisfy his want of warmth and cooking food. Since then fire has been utilised in various directions in the progress of civilisation. Man has been upgraded from stone age to bronze age and then to iron age by inventions to satisfy his necessities. Innumerable inventions of science are the outcome of man's necessities. Even computer, the latest wonder of the world, is the product to satisfy our wider necessities. And in our daily life too, all the articles we use are the products of man's endeavour to remove his wants. Medical science has been gifted with necessary inventions to cure our ailments. Even luxuries have been invented to remove some sort of want — want of ease and comfort. In short we can say that most of the great and good things are the products of divine discontent in the mind of man.

24. NONE BUT A FOOL IS ALWAYS RIGHT
OR
FOOLS RUSH IN WHERE ANGELS FEAR TO TREAD

Some people always claim that they are right. Howsoever fanciful, irrelevant or absurd their views may be, they assert they are right. They are not prepared to accept any contradiction. On the other hand, they ignore or hate all other views. As a result they fail to acquire or develop their knowledge. In fact, the first step towards knowledge is the realisation of one's own ignorance. And if someone does not realise his ignorance, how can he acquire knowledge? The ill-fate of a fool is that he does not care for any opinion that differs from what he says and denies all possibilities of learning anything new. He is convinced that others are wrong while he only is right. Consequently he fails to understand what is actually right, and remains confined in his own folly. Moreover, there are some fields where we need to be very cautious to step in. Even the scholars hesitate there. But the fools are so foolish that they rush in to ruin themselves.

25. ONE MAN'S FOOD IS ANOTHER MAN'S POISON

The needs and tastes vary from man to man. Every requirement, if it is met properly at proper time, has its own worth. In this way what is luxury for one may be a necessity for another, and vice versa. If you are thirsty and need a drink, a delicious dish of meat may be superfluous to you. A drug of poison may be an antidote to another poison, but it may be fatal to whom who does not need it. To extend this logic further one can say that one man's food is another man's poison. It is true not only for an individual, but also for a nation. Thus a country with surplus manpower is advised to prefer small scale industries and cottage industries while a country lacking manpower may be benefited by adopting large scale industries or heavy industries. Machines may be the 'meat' for an underpopulated country, but they are poison to an overpopulated country. Thus, the proverb indicates that what is conducive to one's ability and interest may be detrimental to another in different contexts.

26. ONE HOUR OF A GLORIOUS LIFE IS WORTH AN AGE WITHOUT A NAME

The greatness of a man's life does not depend upon the number of years he spends in this world. It depends upon his achievements. How large is the number of people who die at the ripe age of eighty on ninety. But how many of them are remembered? On the contrary, who can forget Shelley or Keats who died in their young age, but enriched English literature and brought joy to millions of readers? There are others in different directions. Shankaracharya or Swami Vivekananda did not live a long life, but enjoyed an immortal life. Surely one lives in deeds, and not in years. And these deeds may be in any profession. Beginning life as a first-rate shoe-shine boy is more creditable than beginning life as a third-rate engineer. The first one may have a good stand in his profession, while the second one will keep rotting in his office for ever. Even more, he may be responsible for collapsing of a bridge or a building. Likewise, an honest shopkeeper can win greater glory than a corrupt minister.

27. OUR SWEETEST SONGS ARE THOSE THAT TELL OF SADDEST THOUGHT

We seek happiness in our life. But a few men are endowed with it, while most others are not. As it is designed by nature, human life is a complex fabric of weal and woe. And it is largely full of sufferings, disappointments and hardships. We learn more from our sufferings than from our happiness. Our soul gets purified by sufferings, as gold by fire. There are usually more tears than smiles. And tears touch us more deeply than laughter and fun. What touches the heart has, therefore, a more lasting and profound impression than purely momentary enjoyment. Thus the emotional appeal of a tragedy is far more deeper than that of a comedy. Shelley has caught this aspect of human life in immortal expression in a famous line of his poem. It is a paradox that though man loves happiness and shuns sorrows in his daily life, his sympatty goes with the sufferings. Thus songs or other creations of art which deal with a tragic theme evoke much quicker response from human hearts than the lighter subjects. Since sorrows and sufferings are the inevitable lot of human beings, their expression in song or verse have naturally a poignant sweetness for them.

28. PEACE HATH HER VICTORIES NO LESS RENOWNED THAN WAR

Great conquerers like Alexander left an imprint in the pages of history. They brought glory to themselves and victory to their country. The world has faced two Great Wars and some short wars before and after that. Now it is the time to cry not for war, but for peace. We should realise that a period of war is a period of chaos and confusion. On the other hand, development of civilisation embracing arts and science depends on peaceful condition of a country. Architecture, sculpture, painting, music, philosophy, literature, agriculture and even trade and industry owe their birth, growth, and nourishment to peace. These creative gifts of peace are far more lasting than the gifts of war. Hence we want peace, not war; we want amity, not enmity : we want fine arts, not firearms; we want flowering fields, not the desert of destruction — then only can we can gift a better world to our future generations.

29. PREVENTION IS BETTER THAN CURE

It is wiser to avoid a disease by following a healthy measure than to succumb to it and then seek remedies. Moreover, prevention is less costly than cure. Figuratively, the maxim is applicable in a broader sense. Human life is entangled with numerous difficulties. And, therefore, every conscientious man should try to avoid them as much as possible and leave a peaceful life. We know man is distinguished from the lower animals by his power of reasoning. He has the power of foresight, and can utilise it for his own benefit. It would be foolishness to incite difficulties, and, then try to overcome them. Instead of awaiting and facing the troubles, it is better to be on the safe side. Hence, what we need is just to calculate the difficulty and adopt some means to avoid it. Life is short, and, if a considerable part of it is taken up in inviting troubles and then curing them, how will man manage to live a life worth the name? Economy is the law of the day, and it must be applied to every aspect of life. If the above principle is strictly and faithfully followed, much physical and mental suffering can be avoided, and a considerable amount of expense need not be incurred.

30. PROSPERITY GAINS FRIENDS, ADVERSITY TRIES THEM

It is a wholesome proverb. It reveals the great truth about our associations. We see that friends gather around us when we are in prosperity. They can share our richness, happines and luxury and that is profitable to them. But when we face adversity, most of those friends leave us as they cannot find any worldly profit from us at that time. Rather, they are afraid that we may seek some sort of help from them. They are like weather-cocks and face the favourable wind. In this situation we can recognize who are our true friends and who are false friends. We should know that our life is not a comfortable bed of roses for ever. It is mixed with weal and woe. It is the plan of God. Prosperity often makes us luxurious and proud. Adversity makes us patient and diligent. Prosperity makes us callous to others' suffering. Adversity makes us modest and sympathetic. Hardships brings our inner strength and forms our character.

31. SWEET ARE THE USES OF ADVERSITY

It is a famous statement made by the Duke senior in Shakespeare's *As you Like It*. It contains a deep truth of human life. In fact, life is a complex fabric of weal and woe. Happines itself will be meaningless if there is no suffering, nothing contrary to it. Flowers are pretty in contrast with the thorns. Thus adversity, by contrast, enhances the pleasure of prosperity. Prosperity gains friends, adversity tries them. Besides, adversity can sometimes prove itself to be highly beneficial to mankind. It teaches us to face the circumstances with greater courage and confidence. It also develops a man's power of sympathy with the suffering humanity. He who has never suffered can never realise what suffering is. The value of tears can be appreciated only by a man who has to shed tears himself. Adversity also purifies a man. We know that gold gets purified when it is melted in fire. God throws us into deep water not always to drown us, but to wash us clean. Thus adversity provides a man with an opportunity to test his sincerity. It can be really useful to him provided he has a positive attitude towards life.

32. SMALL BEGINNINGS MAKE GREAT ENDINGS
OR
MANY A LITTLE MAKE A MICKLE/MANY A PENNY MAKES A POUND

Every great thing has a small beginning. We know Rome was not built in a day. It took centuries of patient labour and hard toil to bring it to perfection. Even the ocean constitutes innumerable drops of water and a desert is the accumulation of uncountable particles of sand. The proverb is a caution to impatient workers who are not steady to reach the goal. These men begin a thing one day and expect to see its completion the very next morning. And when they see that the work is not actually done within the short time, they lose heart and give it up. The proverb also teaches us that the first thing needed for success of an enterprise is patience. We cannot climb up a mountain with one leap. The summit is reached by slow and cautious steps, and it takes considerable time to get there. Everything is done step by step. The next thing required for success is perseverance. We may face failure at any step. Yet we can achieve success if we can overcome the failures with patience.

33. SCIENCE IS A GOOD SERVANT BUT A BAD MASTER

We live in an age of science. We feel the influence of science at every moment. Science has made its way in almost every sphere of life. It has made our life easy and comfortable. Indeed, modern civilisation is based on the gifts of science. Wherever we cast our eyes, we see the achievements of science—industry, commerce, communication, medicine, and what not. We take the advantages of science from dawn to night. Yet there are some abuses of science. Science has not only invented a robot, but has turned a man into a robot in some cases. Charlie Chaplin said in 'The Great Dictator': "In this age of scientific inventions we think too much, we feel too little." It snatches the soul of a man when he runs into a race in mad pursuit of material prosperity. But science cannot be blamed for this. We can use fire for cooking our food, or burning others' houses. It is not the fault of fire, but of its users. Likewise, man is responsible for the abuses of science. It fully depends on us whether we shall have science to destroy our creation, or to conquer hunger, poverty and disease for a happy and prosperous world.

34. THE SLOW BUT STEADY WINS THE RACE
OR
ROME WAS NOT BUILT IN A DAY

Rome was once the greatest city in the world. But the city did not become so great within a short time. It took centuries of patient labour and hard toil to bring it to perfection. The proverb is a caution to impatient workers who are not steady to reach the goal. These men begin a thing one day and expect to see its result the very next morning. And when they see that the work is not actually done within the short time, they lose heart and give it up. The proverb also teaches us that the first requisite factor for success of an enterprise is patience. We cannot climb up a mountain with one leap. The summit is reached by slow and cautious steps, and it takes considerable time to get there. Everything is done step by step. The next thing required for success is perseverance. We may face failures at any step. Yet we can achieve success if we can overcome the failures with patience. And when our energy fails us, we should remember that Rome was not built in a day. This will infuse fresh vigour and energy into us. This can remind us of another proverb "The slow but steady wins the race."

35. THE CHILD IS THE FATHER OF MAN

This is a paradoxical statement. And though it appears self-contradictory, it contains a profound truth. Like the above statement in Wordsworth's poem *The Rainbow*, Milton also once said, "The child shows the man as the morning shows the day." Exceptions are, of course, there. A day beginning with a bright morning might end in a storm. But those exceptions are very rare. On the other hand, the statement under reference is a general rule. It means that the conduct of a child indicates what he will be in adulthood. Just as the weather of the day is judged from the morning, so the conduct of the child is taken as an indication of what his character will be when he will grow later on. The young mind is very susceptible to impression, good or bad. And such impressions will last throughout one's life. It is, therefore, very important to bring up a child in such a manner that his character may be given the desired bent. We must not forget—one's essential personality always remains what it promises to be in one's childhood.

36. THE HAND THAT ROCKS THE CRADLE RULES THE WORLD

This statement means that mothers are the makers of heroes who rule the world. A mother is the best guide and teacher of a child. The tender heart of a mother always looks to the welfare of a child. She tries to bring up her child very carefully and according to her best ideals. There can be no better well-wisher of a child than its mother, for no one can love it more than she does. But mothers must themselves be noble women in order to be able to shape the future career of their children. Any defect in the mother's character is sure to spoil the child. On the other hand, high-minded, liberal, spirited mothers have made the best children who have ruled over man. It is because a child's mind is very flexible and impressionable. The lives of Napoleon, Iswarchandra Vidyasagar, Vivekananda, Mahatma Gandhi and Netaji

Subhas Chandra Bose, have all been largely shaped by their noble-minded mothers. In this way a mother is said to govern the destiny of the nation. It is she who rocks the cradle and it is she again who rules the world indirectly. And so no nation in the world can hope to be strong and progressive whose women remain uneducated or uncultured.

37. THE OLD ORDER CHANGETH, YIELDING PLACE TO NEW

This line written by Lord Tennyson contains a profound and established truth. In fact, life is nothing but change. Change is the law of Nature. Change stands for eternal freshness and changelessness implies decay. If things were to remain the same, stagnation and destruction would be the result. Stagnant water breeds germs; flowing water remains fresh. An order of things that work well today may prove useless after some time; and then a changed and a new order of things must be allowed to come in gradually. Of course change sometimes comes slowly and silently and we are unaware of the exact moment of its approach. When the change has become fully manifest, it reveals itself to us. This law of change governs the world. And in our societies too conditions are even changing; and unless we adapt ourselves to those conditions, we are bound to suffer. We should remember that without change life is dull and no progress is possible in any way of life. Hence a particular system of state of things passes away, and in its place comes in something new.

38. THE CROWN AND GLORY OF LIFE IS CHARACTER

It is neither power nor money but character alone can bring glory to a man. Power corrupts and breeds bitterness and resentment. Wealth is merely a passing shadow endowing upon man but shadowy glamour. Physical prowess is also basically the attribute of a beast. Only one's character is the crown and glory of life of a man. And character consists of moral courage, discipline and honesty. In a word, it is one's essence, what one really is. And so there is a saying—"When money is lost nothing is lost, when health is lost something is lost; when character is lost everything is lost". All the great men of the world are honoured for their character. Their fields of work may be different, but the basic point is the same. They may be the statesmen or the saints. He may be Gandhiji or Nelson Mandela. He may be Buddha, Christ, Sri Chaitanya or Sri Ramakrishna. Not only that, it is true in case of ordinary people too. An honest shopkeeper is honoured more than a corrupt minister. But character cannot be developed in a day. It takes a long practice of self-exploration and self-discipline to develop one's character.

39. THEY NEVER FAIL WHO DIE IN A GREAT CAUSE

Nobody can even guess—since the beginning of the world, how many have been born, have walked on the surface of the earth and finally died and have been eaten by worms or reduced to ashes. And thus the vast majority left no trace. But even in such an overcrowded world, some noble souls have left their footprints undecayed on the sands of time. It is also seen that all such great men did not necessarily live very long. Some of them died very young. Swami Vivekananda did not live a long life, but he enjoyed an immortal life. Some others again died in ripe age, such as Tolstoy or Tagore. But that is not the real concern. The moot point is how and what for he died. Surely one lives in deeds, and not in years. There are glaring examples who laid down their lives for a great cause and became immortal, while majority of the people are forgotten within a few years. The reason for this is not far to seek. They became immortal because they died for a great cause.

40. THOSE WHO LIVE IN GLASSHOUSES SHOULD NOT THROW STONES AT OTHERS

A glasshouse is brittle and may easily crash down if stones are thrown at it. And a person who himself lives in a glasshouse should not throw stones at other's, because it may provoke others to damage his own house too. In the figurative sense the proverb means we should not abuse others as we may get the same by turn. Yet we are often involved in such a wrong way because finding fault with others is a common human weakness. It is one of the most popular pastimes to sit done in idle groups to chat at the shortcomings of others. But while doing so, we hardly realise that we expose ourselves too to criticism and condemnation of others. None of us is born perfect, and faults can be found in each of us in different degrees. So, we should avoid finding fault with others. Paying in the same coin is the rule of our society. Here respect wins respect and hatred breeds hatred. Only prophets have the right to find faults of human life since they do it from love, not from any ill-motive or malice. So far as common people are concerned, it is best to forgive and forget. We should do unto others what we wish to be done by others.

41. TIME AND TIDE WAIT FOR NONE

One can reverse one's clock or stop it, but passing of time cannot be stopped. So we should be careful of utilising the present moment, as both the past and future are beyond our control. In fact, time is a cruel master. It will not spare even a moment. And tide too waits for none. We ought to keep a constant watch and the moment the tide turns in our favour, we ought to take the opportunity. But if the tide recedes while we are looking the other way and fail to steer our ship of life in the right direction, we are bound to be stuck in shallows and slush. No remorse will bring back the tide. So instead of repenting later, we should be watchful of time and tide. We should remember that the creative and formative years of youth, if once allowed to slip away, will never return. So we should seize time as it approaches as an opportunity, and utilise it to the best of our capabilities.

42. TRUTH IS STRANGER THAN FICTION

Fiction is a feigned or a false story; truth is factual. Fiction refers to the realm of romance or imagination; truth can be experimented. Fiction is exotic and strange; truth is familiar. Ironically, however, it is sometimes reverse—truth is sometimes stranger than fiction. We know science is doing some wonders which we could not imagine in our fictions. Computer is such a truth that is now going beyond fiction. Not only that, in our day-to-day life we sometimes see such an event that a fiction-writer will hesitate to follow. Off and on we come across such amazing headlines in the newspapers or TV channels that takes our breath. A baby was found safe and sound after a plane crash causing all other passengers spot death. An old man of ninety could be rescued alive after ten days from the debris of a collapsed building. An old beggar, always dressed in tattered clothes, died and after his death it was found that he had possessed and kept thousands of rupees in his worn-out pillow. These are not the figments of fiction; they are real-life occurrences. And then why should we not say—truth is stranger than fiction?

43. UNEASY LIES THE HEAD THAT WEARS THE CROWN

This line is taken from Shakespeare's play 'King Henry IV' and is spoken by the king. It suggests that the king's head is so full of worries that he cannot get even a wink of sleep. They live in constant fear of external and internal enemies. Whenever they have to go anywhere, they are heavily guarded. In fact, this is the fate of every one who wears the crown. Though there are no more kings today, yet the proverb continues to hold good. Now the king stands for a person with power and authority and the crown stands for responsibility. The modern Prime Ministers, or Presidents or the Dictators of different countries of the world are also like the kings of the past. Their minds too are burdened with worries. They are always confronted with difficulties and problems. They move from place to place and country to country to solve baffling political and economic problems. Hence, a person who carries some responsibilities is bound to bear some worries. Otherwise, their fate is the inglorious death of a tyrant dictator!

44. VIRTUE IS ITS OWN REWARD

Reward is an incentive to one's work. Man usually works in expectation of a reward. This is the general system. But virtue should not be practised in the hope of gaining any material reward. A noble man, by virtue of his noble spirit, never indulges in petty tricks that bring material benefits. He cannot deceive, he cannot betray, he cannot exploit. Rather, he himself, in many cases, becomes the victim of exploitation. But he always enjoys a spiritual bliss. Virtue brings him mental peace and happiness. On the contrary, a wicked man, unless he is too thick-skinned, will be torn by acute inner conflict or guilty-conscience. He is always afraid of social disapproval and legal penalties. But a virtuous man is never ruffled by any such tensions. Bacon is right when he says, "... the noblest reward of virtue is virtue itself; and the extreme punishment of vice is vice itself."

45. WHERE THERE IS A WILL THERE IS A WAY

"Where there is a will, there is a way" is a very practical maxim. It is a message of hope and encouragement. There are two types of men in our society. One strong-minded, and the other feeble-minded. The strong ones work with a resolute will and overcome the difficulties to achieve glorious success. The feeble ones keep on building fancy castles in the air and achieve nothing. We know the way to success is strewn with numerous obstacles, but resolute minds can overcome them with perseverance. Once Napoleon had to cross the Alps in winter. The mountain was covered with snow. Someone pointed out to Napoleon that it was impossible to cross the Alps at that time. But Napoleon gravely replied that the word 'impossible' was found only in the dictionary of the fools and ordered his soldiers to march on. The soldiers obeyed him and conquered the Alps. So we see there is always a way to do a thing, however difficult, provided there is will. If we make up our minds to accomplish a definite object, we are almost sure to succeed. If we make a sincere attempt and fail, there is nothing to regret. Failures are the pillars of success. We may fail once or twice, but if we work hard with determination, we cannot but be successful in the long run.

PARAGRAPHS
ON
SITUATIONAL TOPICS

1. RESCUING A DROWNING BOY

❑ **Suppose, you had once saved a drowning boy in a river. Describe your experience.**

It was 15th July. I went to the river for taking my bath at 9 am as usual. The bathing ghat was not crowded then. Only two boys were bathing in the river at that time. Suddenly one of them was carried by the fast-flowing current in deep water and cried out for help. The other boy was quite puzzled and stood helplessly. Instantly I made up my mind and dived into the water. I had learnt that technique of rescuing a drowning man in our social service class. So I took the drowning boy by his hair and brought him safely to the shore. In the meantime, some people came there and when they noticed how I rescued the boy, they praised me very much. I thanked my teacher for teaching me how to rescue a drowning man. When my parents heard this, they felt very proud of me.

2. COTTAGE ON FIRE

❑ **Suppose, you had witnessed a cottage on fire and you requested a young man to rescue a girl and an old woman in the burning cottage. Describe your experience.**

Last Sunday I went to bed at 10.30 pm and fell into a sound sleep. Suddenly I woke up at about 12.30 pm when I heard a hue and cry at a little distance. I got up from bed and rushed to the spot. I saw that a cottage was burning. People were rushing towards it. The old woman and the poor little girl who lived in it could not come out. They were crying for help inside the cottage. Everybody was throwing water on the burning cottage but nobody dared to enter the room. At last I requested a brave young man to rescue the old woman and the little girl. My eyes were full of tears then. He looked at my face once again and suddenly rushed into the cottage. He came out with the little girl by his arm and the old lady on his back. I thanked God and felt very happy for the noble deed the young man did. It will be a treasure in my memory for a long time.

3. A PRESSURE COOKER BURST

❑ **You heard a bursting sound at the flat just above your own flat. You rushed there and found the topsy-turvy kitchen as the pressure cooker on the oven had burst.**

Last evening I suddenly heard a bursting sound at the flat just above our flat. At first I hesitated a little as it is our flat culture not to probe one's nose into another's affairs. And at the same time I felt a prick of conscience. I made up my mind and rushed there. I rang the bell and the maid-servant opened the door. Entering the flat I enquired what was the matter—what was the bursting sound. Aunt Molly said the pressure cooker on the oven had burst. Perhaps the saftety vulve did not work properly. The upper part of the cooker had gone off and rebumped from the ceiling. And the meat which was cooking in the pot had strewn on the floor of the kitchen. However, none was hurt seriously. Only a piece of hot meat had fallen on her left foot and she felt a strong burning sensation. I washed her spot on the foot with coconut oil and consoled her it would be easy after a while. It was an accidental and at the same time a memorable incident indeed.

4. LEAKAGE IN THE GAS CYLINDER

❑ **You heard a mild hissing sound from the gas cylinder in your kitchen. What did you do then?**

I was doing my home-task in my study. Mother entered in hasty steps. I was a little surprised. She said, "Come to the kitchen. I'm afraid of a hissing sound from the gas cylinder." Instantly I stepped into the kitchen. I tried to feel any hissing sound from the cylinder and I could smell gas. After a few minutes I was sure the gas cylinder is leaking mildly. Immediately I rang to the gas centre and informed the matter. They responded quickly. Within half an hour a man from the centre came to the spot. He checked the cylinder and found the fault. He said he could stop the fault temporarily, but it is better to change it. We agreed. And he took off the faulty cylinder and sent a fresh one within the next half an hour. We all felt a sense of relief as it is occasionally heard of bursting gas cylinder causing accident.

5. SUITCASE LEFT ON THE LUGGAGE RACK IN TRAIN

❑ **You have got off a train at a station and after the train has started you find that you have left your suitcase on the luggage rack. What would you do?**

I always suffer from absent-mindedness. Only the other day I fell into a precarious situation. I was travelling by a train and kept my suitcase on the luggage rack. And when the train approached the halt station, I got off the train and began to chitchat with a friend who had come to receive me. When the train whistled and started to move out of the platform, I suddenly remembered that I had left my suitcase on the luggage rack of the train. A chill feeling passed through my spine. The first thought that flashed to mind was to jump on to the running train, grab my suitcase, and jump back and be relieved. But the next moment I thought it would be risky. My friend suggested to approach the station master and give him a plausible explanation of my folly furnishing the details of my suitcase. I went to him and requested him to contact the station master of the next station so that my suitcase could be retrieved. And it was.

6. SUITCASE LEFT IN A TAXI

❑ **You have lost your suitcase containing valuables while travelling by a taxi. Going to the local police station you met the taxi-driver ready to return your suitcase. Describe your experience.**

Last Sunday I was returning from Gariahat market by a taxi. I had made some valuable purchases like Benarasi sari and a box of ornaments for my sister's marriage next week. Coming to the front door of our home, I got down from the taxi taking the packet of Benarasi sari in my hand. When my mother enquired of the ornaments, I at once rushed to the road. But by that time the taxi-driver had left the place. I was sure the valuable ornaments were lost for good. However, I went to the local police station to make a diary of the loss. But I found that the taxi driver was standing there with the box of ornaments in one hand! He at once identified me and returned the box. I gained a positive experience of the honesty of the taxi driver in this age of erosion of values. Still another surprise was waiting for me. I wanted to reward the man Rs. 1,000 but he politely refused to take it. He said it was his duty and he could not claim any reward for it. Just think of the rare virtue of a common man! Such men and such behaviour redeem our faith on fellow-feeling and humanity.

7. A PICKPOCKET IN A BUS

❑ **The conductor of a bus asked you to buy ticket. As you put your hand in your pocket you realised that your purse was missing. Describe your experience.**

Last Monday I waited at the bus stop to catch my bus. And when it came, it was already over-crowded. With great difficulty I managed to board on it, but I was forced to keep standing at the gate for some time. A good number of passengers were also standing there and I was almost sandwiched between two fat persons. Somehow I managed to squeeze myself through the crowd to find a little breathing space. In the meantime the conductor approached me to buy my ticket. I told him to give me a seven-rupee ticket. I put my hand in my pocket to take out my wallet, but I was shocked to see that it was missing. However, I gained courage and shouted that my purse had been stolen by someone. Some passengers caught a suspected one and my purse was found with him as it was easily detected with my voter I D card. When the public tried to give him a good thrash, I suggested to hand him over to the police.

8. HOUSE BURGLED

❑ **Returning from a tour to South India for fifteen days with your family you found your house had been burgled. Describe your experience.**

We enjoyed a family tour to South India for fifteen days. We came back to our flat last evening, anticipating a night of refreshing rest. But to our utter surprise we noticed that our front door was unlocked. We pushed the door open and stepped in. The scene inside was quite unnerving. The burglar had ransacked all the rooms and taken away whatever valuables they could get. My laptop was gone. They had robbed of all my mother's jewellery. My sister could not find her costly camera. The almirah in my father's room was also broken and the cash, the pass book and cheque book and some share certificates were gone. Immediately we informed the local police station. And within an hour the police came and made a prima-facie enquiry. They assured us that they will be able to catch the gang and we had nothing to do but to wait and rely on them.

9. TAXI BROKE DOWN ON THE WAY

❑ **You were going to appear for your final examination, and the taxi broke down on the way. Describe your experience.**

I hired a taxi as I was going to appear at my final examination. The distance from my home to the examination centre was about 4 km. But unfortunately I had hardly covered 1 km when the taxi broke down. The driver tried to restart the vehicle, but failed. The fear of being late at the examination began to torment me. No other taxi was in sight. I could not determine what to do at that precarious moment. Presently there appeared a man on a motorbike. At first he showed his reluctance to oblige me, but when I explained to him the urgency of the matter, he agreed to drop me at the place of my examination. I was only five minutes late when I reached there. I thanked the gentleman, took some water from my bottle and felt at ease. Then I tried to concentrate my mind on the question paper.

10. FEELINGS WHILE SHIFTING RESIDENCE

❑ **Describe a time when you had to shift residence. How did you feel? As you look back to that time, do you feel nostalgic?**

We had been living in a rented house for more than 15 years. But the landlord sold the house to a promoter and we had to shift our residence on another part of the town in three months' notice. There were lots of things of the household. Father hired a matador for shifting the things. But mother was puzzled what to take and what to leave. I was arranging my books and the laptop to take with me. The almirah containing the valuables was put on the matador. But most of the large furniture were sold cheap. I was upset when my reading table was gone. It was my companion for more than ten years. Mother could not but shed her tears while stepping out of the house. Father was busy with the work of shifting. I was helping him in that work. But when we got into the vehicle and the driver started, I could not check my emotion. Entering our new flat, I, however, thought that it was not so bad. And gradually we are now becoming accustomed to the new surroundings. Yet at times I feel nostalgic when the old house and the bosom friends of that neighbourhood flash in my mind.

KEY TO
GRAMMAR EXERCISES

KEY TO GRAMMAR EXERCISES

CHAPTER 1 : SENTENCE CONSTRUCTION

EXERCISE 1

Ratan is a good cricketer.

The boys are playing in the playground.

The girls are dancing in the hall.

The cows are grazing in the field.

The birds are flying in the sky.

EXERCISE 2

(i)	Mary—**Subject**	has a little lamb—**Predicate**
(ii)	She—**Subject**	has a good memory—**Predicate**
(iii)	The boy—**Subject**	stood on the burning deck—**Predicate**
(iv)	The earth—**Subject**	moves round the sun—**Predicate**
(v)	Nature—**Subject**	is the best physician—**Predicate**
(vi)	All roads—**Subject**	lead to Rome—**Predicate**
(vii)	A barking dog—**Subject**	seldom bites—**Predicate**
(viii)	We—**Subject**	cannot pump the ocean dry—**Predicate**
(ix)	Edison—**Subject**	invented the photograph—**Predicate**
(x)	We—**Subject**	should profit by ourselves—**Predicate**

CHAPTER 2 : KINDS OF SENTENCES AND THEIR FUNCTIONS

EXERCISE 1

1. Assertive 2. Interrogative 3. Imperative 4. Optative 5. Exclamatory

EXERCISE 2

1. Statement 2. Order/Command 3. Question 4. Desire 5. Emotion

EXERCISE 3

(i) Asserting a fact (ii) Denying a fact (iii) Asking for information (iv) Giving information (v) Stating a fact (vi) Denying a fact (vii) Giving information (viii) Requesting (ix) Hesitating (x) Giving information (xi) Supposing (xii) Giving opinion (xiii) Giving a statement (xiv) Enquiring (xv) Asserting a fact (xvi) Giving opinion (xvii) Giving opinion (xviii) Requesting (xix) Asking for confirmation (xx) Asking for information (xxi) Stating a fact (xxii) Giving suggestion (xxiii) Enquiring (xxiv) Giving a suggestion (xxv) Exclamation (xxvi) Expressing a situation (xxvii) Expressing a decision (xxviii) Stating a fact (xxix) Enquiring (xxx) Requesting (xxxi) Asking for permission (xxxii) Order/Command (xxxiii) Expressing ability.

EXERCISE 4

(i) Yes, I admit it./I agree to your proposal.

(ii) What are you doing now?/Where are you going?

(iii) Her virtues are : sincerity, punctuality, and truthfulness.

(iv) Faruk cannot do this, can he?

(v) I don't like these cheap materials.

(vi) Our next semester will begin on coming Friday.

(vii) You can do wonders if you work sincerely.

(viii) I'm not sure what will be the result.

(ix) I'll look into the matter today.

(x) Today is a holiday, isn't it?

(xi) The building caught fire and the inhabitans shouted for help.

(xii) The employee appealed to the authority for getting a promotion.

(xiii) I must take the challenge.

(xiv) Yes, I'll finish the job within a week.

(xv) Please give me a cup of tea.

(xvi) He is not a thief, is he?

(xvii) The boy was crying on the street; he had lost this parents.

(xviii) What a nice landscape!

(xix) You must do your homework regularly.

(xx) You have appropriately dealt with the matter.

(xxi) First break the egg to prepare an omlette.

(xxii) He has been fired by the authority.

(xxiii) No, I can't take the fish at such a high price.

(xxiv) You can go to Big Bazar to get your choice.

(xxv) You have done your part perfectly.

(xxvi) Do you think the couple will be happy?

(xxvii) You may be sacked for such negligence of duty.

(xxviii) You may take this medicine for your backache.

(xxix) You must give up smoking; it is risky for your health.

(xxx) What a nuisance! The street dog is on the busy road.

(xxxi) The poor street dog has got nothing to eat.

(xxxii) Go on! I'm sure you will win the prize.

(xxxiii) I'll lend you the money if you repay it within a month.

(xxxiv) Kindly grant me a leave for three days.

CHAPTER 3 : PARTS OF SPEECH

EXERCISE 1

1. Each word is actually a part of our speech; hence all types of words are called parts of speech according to their use.

EXERCISE 2

There are eight kinds of parts of speech:

Noun : boy, book, class, gold
Pronoun : I, you, he, she, They
Adjective : good, bad, much, many
Verb : is, have, do, play
Adverb : ago, idly, surely
Preposition : at, in, on, behind
Conjunction : and, but, or, otherwise
Interjection : Hello, Alas, Hurrah, Bravo

EXERCISE 3

Noun	Pronoun	Verb	Adjective	Adverb
father, mother	you, we	break, burn	hot, cold	again, ago
brother, sister	his, she	ask, keep	beautiful,	daily, early
boy, girl	they	learn, teach	ugly, kind	often, never
		stand, sleep	cruel, red	always, idly
		swim, dance	white	openly
		write, weave		surely

EXERCISE 4

Preposition	Conjunction	Interjection
across, to	as, or, but, and	Ah, Oh, Alas
into, through, below	if, both, else	Hurrah, Help
under, up, over	lest, for, till	Bravo, Fie
above, between		Hush, Hark
among, with, within		Goodbye
without, towards		
before, after, by, behind		
beyond, from, of, upon, on		

EXERCISE 5

(i) **honesty** (ii) **intelligence** (iii) **kindness** (iv) **me** (v) **swimming** (vi) **walking** (vii) **Indian** (viii) **tasteful** (ix) **healthy** (x) **beautifully**

EXERCISE 6

(a) Abdul—**Noun**, and—**Conjunction**, Latif—**Noun**, are—**Verb,** brothers—**Noun**

(b) Delhi—**Noun,** is—**Verb**, a—**Determiner (article)**, Great—**Adjective**

(c) The—**Determiner**, clothes—**Noun**, have been washed—**Verb**, with—**Preposition**, soap—**Noun**

(d) The—**Determiner**, girl—**Noun**, has—**Verb**, a—**Adjective (Determiner),** Voice—**Noun**

(e) Debkumar—**Noun**, is—**Verb**, The—**Determiner**, first—**Adjective**, boy—**Noun**, in—**Preposition**, the—**Determiner**, class—**Noun**

(f) Columbus—**Noun**, discovered—**Verb**, America—**Noun**

(g) Solomon—**Noun**, was—**Verb**, famous—**Adjective**, for—**Preposition**, his—**Pronoun**, wisdom—**Noun**

(h) He—**Pronoun**, treats—**Verb**, his—**Pronoun**, children—**Noun**, with—**Preposition**, great—**Adjective**, kindness—**Noun**

(i) The—**Determiner**, Wind—**Noun**, and—**Conjunction**, the—**Determiner**, Sun—**Noun**, had—**Verb**, a—**Determiner**, quarrel—**Noun**

(j) The—**Determiner**, showed—**Verb**, great—**Adjective**, courage—**Noun**

(k) Our—**Pronoun (Pronominal Adjective)**, class—**Noun**, consists—**Verb**, of—**Preposition**, forty—**Adjective**, pupils—**Noun**.

(l) The—**Determiner**, girl's—**Adjective**, hair—**Noun**, is—**Verb**, long—**Adjective**, and—**Conjunction**, thick—**Adjective**, and—**Conjunction**, full—**Adjective**, of—**Preposition**, curls—**Noun**

(m) The—**Determiner**, earth—**Noun**, moves—**Verb**, round—**Preposition**, the—**Determiner**, sun—**Noun**, once—**Adverb**, in—**Preposition** a—**Determiner,** Year—**Noun**

(n) Boys,—**Noun**, sometimes—**Adverb**, act—**Verb**, like—**Preposition**, monkeys—**Noun**, in—**Preposition**, their—**Pronoun**, play—**Noun**

(o) The—**Determiner**, stars—**Noun**, shine—**Verb**, through—**Preposition**, the—**Determiner**, branches—**Noun**, of—**Preposition**, he—**Determiner,** tree—**Noun**

(p) A—**Determiner**, boy's—**Adjective**, head—**Noun**, has—**Verb**, less—**Adjective,** than—**Conjunction**, a —**Determiner**, monkey's—**Adjective**

(q) The—**Determiner**, days—**Noun**, are—**Verb**, hotter—**Adjective**, then—**Adverb**, the—**Determiner**, nights—**Noun**

(r) Parents—**Noun**, Must do—**Verb**, their—**Adjective**, duty—**Noun**, to—**Preposition**, their—**Adjective**, children—**Noun**

(s) The—**Determiner**, people—**Noun**, who—**Pronoun**, live—**Verb**, in—**Preposition**, India—**Noun**, are called—**Verb**, Indians—**Noun**

(t) Without—**Preposition**, wealth—**Noun**, there—**Pronoun** (Introductory), is—**Verb**, no—**Adjective**, happiness—**Noun**.

CHAPTER 4 : KINDS OF NOUNS

EXERCISE 1

There are five kinds of Nouns :

Proper Noun : Rahul, Rina, India, Delhi

Common Noun : boy, girl, man, country, city

Collective Noun : army, crowd, class, fleet, jury

Material Noun : gold, silver, coal, wood, water

Abstract Noun : honesty, beauty, kindness, boyhood, wisdom

EXERCISE 2

Proper Noun	Common Noun	Collective Noun	Material Noun	Abstract Noun
Amal, Binod	Father, mother	army, class	gold, silver	truth
Vidyasagar	boy, girl, post-	crowd	iron	wisdom
Solomon,	man, carpenter	bundle		strength
Ramayana	hawker, fruit			unity
Mahabharata	player, club			
	stick, place			
	shoes, chair			
	table, ruler			

EXERCISE 3

(a) Solomon—**Proper Noun** wisdom—**Abstract Noun**

(b) class—**Collective Noun** pupils—**Common Noun**

(c) elephant—**Common Noun** strength—**Abstract Noun**

(d) soldiers—**Common Noun** bravery—**Abstract Noun**

(e) health—**Abstract Noun** happiness—**Abstract Noun**

(f) bunch—**Collective Noun** grapes—**Common Noun**

(g) cows—**Common Noun** grass—**Common Noun**
tigers—**Common Noun** flesh—**Material Noun**

(h) Honey—**Material Noun** milk—**Material Noun**

(i) Cleanliness—**Abstract Noun** godliness—**Abstract Noun**

(j) Wisdom—**Abstract Noun** strength—**Abstract Noun**

EXERCISE 4

(a) laziness length truth freedom poverty
cruelty strength falsehood pride wisdom
youth width goodness novelty humanity

	decency	breadth	darkness	modesty	justness/ justice
	bravery	height	depth	vacancy	similarity
	bitterness	shortage	prudency	sweetness	ignorance
(b)	livelihood	action	choice	death	sight
	obedience	hatred	movement	thought	cleanliness
	laughter	service	seizure	advice	judgement
	knowledge	starvation	flattery	defence	pursuance
	stealing/stealth	pleasure	departure	protection	relief
	excellence	belief	concealment	punishment	conversation
	expectation	occupation	perseverance	success	discovery
(c)	boyhood	infancy	authorship	bondage	friendship
	manhood	womanhood	motherhood	priesthood	enmity
	childhood	ownership	agency	piracy	capitalism
	kingship	roguery	heroism	pilgrimage	patriotism
	theft	regentship	beggary	cowardice	bankruptcy

CHAPTER 5 : COUNTABLE AND UNCOUNTABLE NOUNS

EXERCISE 1

Countable Nouns are those which can be counted.

Examples : boy, girl, book, chair, table

Uncountable Nouns are those which cannot be counted.

Examples : rice, water, milk, salt, sugar

EXERCISE 2

Sentences with 'a few', 'a little', 'many,' and 'much' :

A few boys were late in the class.

I want **a little sugar** in my tea.

Many people attended the meeting.

Much water is wasted in the drinking lines.

EXERCISE 3

Sentences with 'some' :

Some boys are absent-minded.

Some books are good for reading.

Some men are too ambitious.

Some apples are rotten in the basket.

The teacher asked the boy to give **some examples**.

Sentences with 'a lot of' :

Here is a lot of sugar.

There is a lot of salt.

A lot of new books have been purchased.

I have to do a lot of homework.

The company wants a lot of employees.

EXERCISE 4

(a) **a little** (b) **a few** (c) **many** (d) **a few** (e) **much** (f) **much** (g) **much** (h) **a few**

EXERCISE 5

(a) I want much milk.

He wants a little salt.

They want a lot of sugar.

The cat wants many fishes. (different types of fish)

Samir and Dipak want a few chairs.

The naughty boy wants an orange.

The greedy monkey wants a banana.

(b) Is there any milk?

Is there much sugar?

Is there some rice?

Is there a lot of wheat?

Are there many boys?

(c) How much money is there?

How much water is there?

How much milk is there?

How many pens are there?

How many boys are there?

How many books are there?

CHAPTER 6 : THE NOUN : NUMBER

EXERCISE 1

There are two types of numbers in English—(1) Singular Number, and (2) Plural Number.

Singular Number : boy, book, ass, bamboo, hero, army, calf, chief, man, mouse, ox, son-in-law, man-servant

Plural Number : boys, books, asses, bamboos, heroes, armies, calves, chiefs, men, mice, oxen, sons-in-law, men-servants

EXERCISE 2

Singular	Plural	Singular	Plural	Singular	Plural
Boy	Boys	Knife	Knives	Leaf	Leaves
Bus	Buses	Life	Lives	Chief	Chiefs
Comb	Combs	Man	Men	Child	Children
City	Cities	Woman	Women	mouse	Mice
Country	Countries	Fisherman	Fishermen	Son-in-law	Sons-in-law
Fool	Fools	Gentleman	Gentlemen	Step-brother	Step-brothers
Foot	Feet	Calf	Calves	Man-servant	Men-servants
Tooth	Teeth	Roof	Roofs	Passer-by	Passers-by
Eye	Eyes	Hero	Heroes	Sheep	Sheep
Ear	Ears	Radio	Radios	Railway	Railways
Baby	Babies	Bamboo	Bamboos	Valley	Valleys
Thief	Thieves	Body	Bodies	Volcano	Volcanoes.

EXERCISE 3

Singular	Plural	Singular	Plural
Air—wind	Airs—manners	Force—power	Forces—army
Good—well-being	Goods—things	Iron—a kind of metal	Irons—chains
Sand—a kind of matter	Sands—desert	Wood—timber	Woods—forest

EXERCISE 4

Singular	Plural	Singular	Plural
Brother	Brother — sons of same parents Brethren — members of the same society	Fish	Fish — collectively fish Fishes — fishes of different types
Cloth	cloths — pices of cloth clothes — garments	Genius	Geniuses — men of talent Genii — spirits

EXERCISE 5

Singular	Plural	Singular	Plural
Deer	Deer	Dozen	Dozen
Sheep	Sheep	Score	Score
Pice	Pice	Hundred	Hundred
Public	Public	Thousand	Thousand

EXERCISE 6

(a) children (b) women (c) teeth (d) boys (e) deer (f) pice

CHAPTER 7 : THE NOUN : GENDER

EXERCISE 1

Masculine		Feminine	Common	Neuter
cock	master	aunt	baby	chair
man	priest	wife	doctor	table
hero	lord	niece	teacher	book
brother	male	bride	tutor	pen
son	host	—	—	oil
poet	—	—	—	rice
prince	—	—	—	—
tiger	—	—	—	—

EXERCISE 2

Father—mother, boy—girl, daughter—son, husband—wife
uncle—aunt, hero—heroine, master—mistress, widow—widower
man—woman, nephew—niece, sir—madam, brother—sister
mother-in-law—father-in-law, milkman—milk-woman, host—hostess
bride—bridegroom, tiger—tigress, lion—lioness, man-servant—maid-servant
grandfather—grandmother

EXERCISE 3

(a) Arthur is my brother.

(b) Meera is my sister.

(c) Byron is a great poet.

(d) Akbar was a great king.

(e) The cow gives us milk.

CHAPTER 8 : THE NOUN : CASE

EXERCISE 1

(a) Ram, (b) Milk, (c) Gopal, (d) boy, (e) Kolkata; (f) earth

EXERCISE 2

(a) way, (b) meal, (c) Ramayana, (d) cottage girl, (e) lamp, (f) hair

EXERCISE 3

(a) baby's, (b) girl's, (c) boys', (d) girls', (e) children's, (f) ladies'

EXERCISE 4

Singular	Plural	Singular	Plural
man's	men's	child's	children's
boy's	boys'	sheep's	sheep's
baby's	babies'	deer's	deer's
lady's	ladies'	ox's	oxen's

EXERCISE 5

(a) Parents' kindness, (b) A man's labour, (c) Authors' books

(d) A student's books (e) A king's crown, (f) The journey's end

CHAPTER 9 : MORE ABOUT PRONOUNS

EXERCISE 1

There are ten different kinds of pronouns.

They are : Personal Pronoun, Impersonal Pronoun,
Possessive Pronoum, Indefinite Pronoun, Distributive Pronoun,
Reciprocal Pronoun, Interrogative Pronoun, Relative Pronoun

EXERCISE 2

NUMBER AND CASE OF PERSONAL PRONOUN

Person	Number	Subject [Nominative]	Object [Objective]	Possessive
1st person	**Singular**	I	me	my, mine
	Plural	We	us	our, ours
2nd person	**Singular**	You	you	your, yours
	Plural	You	you	your, yours
3rd person	**Singular**	He, She	him, her	his, her, hers
	Plural	They	them	their, theirs

Note : Though basically Pronouns, **my**, **our**, **your**, **his**, **her** and **their** are Possessive Adjectives for their function.

EXERCISE 3

An Interrogative Pronoun such as who, whom, whose, which, what is used to ask questions.

But a Relative Pronoun such as who, whom, whose, which, what is used to relate its antecedent.

Interrogative Pronoun : Who are you?

Relative Pronoun : I know the boy who stood first.

EXERCISE 4

They—Personal Pronoun; their—Possessive Pronoun; Which—Interrogative Pronoun; Your—Pronominal Adjective; Yours—Possessive Pronoun; I—Personal Pronoun; him—Personal Pronoun; he—Personal Pronoun; it—Impersonal Pronoun; Any—Indefinite Pronoun; somebody—Indefinite Pronoun; I—Personal Pronoun; myself—Reflexive Pronoun; He—Personal Pronoun; himself—Reflex Pronoun; who—Interrogative Pronoun; you—Personal Pronoun; what—Interrogative Pronoun; Each—Distributive Pronoun; Either—Distributive Pronoun; them—Personal Pronoun; It—Impersonal Pronoun; each other—Reciprocal Pronoun

EXERCISE 5

A farmer had three sons who always quarrelled. They made the farmer unhappy. One day the farmer thought of a plan. He called in all his sons. He showed a bundle of sticks and asked them to break the bundle. All his sons tried but no one could break it.

EXERCISE 6

his—Possessive Pronoun (Pronominal Adjective); She—Personal Pronoun; ours—Possessive Pronoun; your—Possessive Pronoun (Pronominal Adjective); It—Impersonal Pronoun; me—Personal Pronoun.

EXERCISE 7

(a) I, (b) I, my, (c) he, (d) their, (e) her, (f) me, your

EXERCISE 8

(a) that—Relative Pronoun in Objective case; antecedent—pen
(b) (that/which omitted) Relative Pronoun in Objective case; antecedent—ball
(c) which—Relative Pronoun in Objective case; antecedent—answer
(d) whose—Relative Pronoun in Possessive case; antecedent—woman
(e) whom—Relative Pronoun in Objective case; antecedent—boy
(f) which—Relative Pronoun in Objective case; antecedent—letters
(g) that—Relative Pronoun in Objective case; antecedent—house
(h) that—Relative Pronoun in Objective case; antecedent—knife
(i) that—Relative Pronoun in Objective case; antecedent—knife

EXERCISE 9

(a) We always like those boys who speak the truth.
(b) He who does his best shall be praised.
(c) We saw the dog that/which worried the cat.
(d) I know what you mean.
(e) Most people want what they deserve.

(f) Where is the book that I gave you?

(g) God helps those who help themselves.

(h) No man can lose what he never had.

EXERCISE 10

(a) This is the boy who got the first prize.

(b) This is the building that/which was built in a month.

(c) The letter which you sent reached me this evening.

(d) The dog that barks does not bite.

(e) This is the man whom I want.

(f) This is the girl whose book is lost.

(g) I have found the umbrella which I had lost.

(h) The boy who came to me yesterday is your classmate.
[or] The boy who is your classmate came to me yesterday.

(i) The film is about a spy whose wife betrays him.

(j) Do you know the boys who were absent?

EXERCISE 11

1. Here is the book which you lent me.
2. I met a lame man who was walking in the field.
3. The man is the secretary whom you see on the chair.
4. Is this the road that leads to the station?
5. I gave the baby the doll whose head was off.

EXERCISE 12

Where did the boy live?/Did the boy live at Bhawanipur in Kolkata?

Where did his parents send him?/Did his parents send him to school?

Who is the king of football?/Is Pele the king of football?

How old is Dipak?/Is Dipak 14 years old?

What is his father?/Is his father a teacher?

What have you seen in the garden?/Have you seen some birds in the garden?

Whom did he invite?/Did he invite some friends?

What for is he going? Is he going to buy some books?

CHAPTER 10 : MORE ABOUT ADJECTIVES

EXERCISE 1

(a) Every, (b) same, (c) long, cold, (d) absent, (e) glorious, (f) Good (g) old, deaf, dumb, (h) few, (i) small, large, (j) tall, (k) Neither, right, (l) Which, (m) much, little.

EXERCISE 2

(a) The first prize was won by Rahim.

(b) The poor woman lives in a wretched hut.

(c) This is a very important matter.
(d) There were riots in several places.
(e) Every cloud has a silver lining.
(f) Suddenly arose a violent storm.
(g) He is a man of high ambition.
(h) He always walks with a slow step.
(i) Have you any reason for leaving the country?
(j) The Battle of Waterloo ended in a great victory.

EXERCISE 3

active man, **doubtful** case, **healthy** boy, **wealthy** woman, **timely** action, **pitiful** condition, **heavenly** joy, **lovely** scene, **hilly** area, **painful** situation, **wonderful** sight, **peaceful** atmosphere, **childish** behaviour, **thoughtful** man, **hopeful** condition, **friendly** dealings, **quarrelsome** woman, **stormy** weather, **starry** sky, **leafy** tree, **sunny** day.

EXERCISE 4

lazy	:	He is a lazy boy.
big	:	This is a big bag.
small	:	That is a small packet.
tall	:	Rakesh is a tall boy.
hard	:	Iron is a hard metal.
sad	:	Why are you so sad?
happy	:	Nobody is always happy.
rude	:	Don't be so rude.
polite	:	Try to be polite in your behaviour.
rich	:	Mukesh is a rich man.
poor	:	A poor beggar is begging on the street.
young	:	Many young men are unemployed.
old	:	The old man has retired from his service.
long	:	Now we have a long way to go.
short	:	Try to answer these short questions.
healthy	:	Early to bed and early to rise makes a man healthy, wealthy and wise.
clever	:	The crow is a clever bird.
cruel	:	The cruel man is beating his pet.
beautiful	:	This is a beautiful flower.
ugly	:	I have never seen such an ugly scene.

EXERCISE 5

Positive	Comparative	Superlative	Positive	Comparative	Superlative
able	abler	ablest	**hot**	hotter	hottest
easy	easier	easiest	**big**	bigger	biggest
early	earlier	earliest	**good**	better	best
busy	busier	busiest	**bad**	worse	worst
strong	stronger	strongest	**weak**	weaker	weakest
short	shorter	shortest	**intelligent**	more intelligent	most intelligent.

EXERCISE 6

He is the worst of all in the class.

He is taller than his sister.

He is more intelligent than his brother.

She is happier than her sister.

You are dearer to me than life.

Iron is the most useful of all metals.

Gold is more valuable than iron.

Fatema is as old as Salma.

She is her father's elder/eldest daughter.

This tree is older than that.

Which do you like better—rain or sunshine?

EXERCISE 7

I want a book of the latest edition.

Reba is elder than her sister.

She has lost much blood.

Nasir has many friends.

He came later than his brother.

I want the former, not the latter.

EXERCISE 8

Mr. Bose is not as old as Mr. Roy.

He has more weight than Mr. Das.

Mr. Roy is taller than Mr. Das, but Mr. Bose is taller than Mr. Roy.

EXERCISE 9

(a) Cricket is more interesting/less exciting than football.

(b) English is less difficult/more interesting than Arithmetic.

(c) A dog is more faithful than a cat.

(d) The rainy season is better/more pleasant than the winter season.

(e) Delhi from Kolkata is farther than Mumbai from Kolkata.

CHAPTER 11 : MORE ABOUT VERBS AND MODALS

EXERCISE 1

(a) I don't think I shall be able to go.
(b) He will not pay unless he is compelled.
(c) You should be punctual.
(d) I wish you must be punctual.
(e) You ought to pay your debts.
(f) Would you please help me with this?
(g) You mustn't light a match; the room is full of gas.
(h) She used to play badminton before her marriage.

EXERCISE 2

(a) Killed—Principal Verb
(b) Do—Auxiliary Verb, Know—Principal Verb
(c) did—Principal Verb
(d) has—Auxiliary Verb, passed—Principal Verb
(e) is—Principal Verb
(f) is—Auxiliary Verb, going—Principal Verb
(g) Do—Auxiliary Verb, laugh—Principal Verb

EXERCISE 3

(a) **shines**—Intransitive Verb
(b) **burns**—Intransitive Verb
(c) **blew**—Transitive Verb (object—whistle)
(d) **blow**—Intransitive Verb
(e) **stood**—Intransitive Verb
(f) **keep**—Transitive Verb (object—time)
(g) **bring**—Transitive Verb (object—camera)
(h) **own**—Transitive Verb (object—reward)
(i) **lifted**—Transitive Verb (object—weight)
(j) **speak**—Transitive Verb (object—languages)

EXERCISE 4

(a) **teach**—Finite Verb; to swim—Non-finite
(b) **made**—Finite Verb; run—Non-finite
(c) **wants**—Finite Verb; to go, to visit—Non-finite
(d) **putting**—Non-finite; went—Finite; to see—Non-finite
(e) **being**—Non-finite; did—Finite Verb

EXERCISE 5

(a) Every cricket team has a captain to direct the other players.
(b) His father went to Delhi to visit Rajghat.

(c) You must part with your purse to save your money.
(d) The robber took out a knife to frighten the old man.
(e) He works hard to earn his livelihood.
(f) He has four children to provide.

EXERCISE 6

(a) The soldier is angry and he is shouting at his enemy.
(b) You should stop before you get into trouble.
(c) By the time he receives this letter, I will be in Japan.
(d) The population of the world is increasing and we must produce more food.
(e) This book belongs to me and you cannot demand it.

EXERCISE 7

(a) The students must submit the assignments within a week.
(b) The government ought to do something about the flood-affected people.
(c) You ought not tell anyone what I said.
(d) He is really needy; you have to help him.
(e) Fatima might hear the sound of music but she couldn't understand the lyric.
(f) You could come here earlier as it may rain today.

EXERCISE 8

(a) It may rain today.
(b) The Indian team can beat Australia.
(c) May I get out of the class for a while?
(d) You should not watch TV for long hours.
(e) You need not (needn't) wait for me.

CHAPTER 12 : SYNTAX : SUBJECT-VERB AGREEMENT

EXERCISE 1

(i) One of the helicopters is missing.
(ii) No news is absolutely good news.
(iii) Neither of the girls is quite at her ease.
(iv) The jury were divided in their opinion.
(v) Each of the robbers is arrested.
(vi) Twenty rupees is too much for this article.
(vii) Two-thirds of the book has been lost.
(viii) Shakespeare is one of the greatest dramatists that have ever lived.
(ix) Which one of these books is yours?
(x) Two tons of coal are here.
(xi) None of the boys has done the sum.

(xii) Iron as well as copper is found in India.
(xiii) The cost of all the necessary articles has risen.
(xiv) The chief with his followers has arrived.
(xv) 'The Arabian Nights' has delighted many generations.
(xvi) None of the girls is/was present in the class.
(xvii) There is/was a large number of boys in the field.
(xviii) A number of boys were found copying.
(xix) Here is a group of boys.
(xx) A group of boys are going on the road.

EXERCISE 2

(i) Time and tide waits for none.
(ii) Early to bed and early to rise makes a man healthy, wealthy and wise.
(iii) Each man and each woman has been given a prize.
(iv) I, and not my brother, have done this.
(v) No man, no woman and no child has been saved.
(vi) Only men and no child are allowed to enter the room.
(vii) Two books only and no pen are required.
(viii) Each boy and each girl is/was present.
(ix) He as well as his friends is/was guilty.
(x) The boys as well as their leader are running away.
(xi) The king with his guards has been killed.
(xii) Mr. Roy, together with his children, is buying some sweets.
(xiii) If I were a king, I would ban examinations.
(xiv) Either you or he has done this.
(xv) Neither life nor property is for ever.
(xvi) Either you or your friends are guilty.
(xvii) You are the man who has done this.
(xviii) The Headmaster and Secretary of the school is coming.
[But] The Headmaster and the Secretary of the school are coming.
(xix) Not only he but also his friends have come here.
(xx) One of the boys is a liar.

CHAPTER 13 : CONJUGATION OF VERBS

EXERCISE 1 & EXERCISE 2 Can be easily done with the help of the reading materials in the textbook.

CHAPTER 14 : TIME AND TENSE WITH MOOD

EXERCISE 1

(i) The earth moves round the sun and the sun gives us light.
(ii) He always buys lottery tickets, but never wins any prize.

(iii) Are you going to school now?

(iv) Have you done your homework?

(v) I have known him for several years.

(vi) I got your letter yesterday.

(vii) He came here last Sunday.

(viii) She does not buy anything from the shopkeeper.

(ix) I was washing my hands when the telephone rang.

(x) I shall telephone you when she comes back.

EXERCISE 2

(i) He was studying when my uncle entered the room.

(ii) I must stay here because I am expecting a parcel.

(iii) I see the price of petrol has gone up recently.

(iv) The kites were flying in the sky before it started raining.

(v) I had been looking for a suitable job before I got this one.

EXERCISE 3

(a) While I was walking back home yesterday, someone snatched the bag from my hand and ran away. The police could not catch him yet. I wonder how such things happen nowadays.

(b) Every particle of matter attracts or pulls every other particle. That is the law of gravitation. The sun attracts the earth and the earth, in turn, attracts the moon.

(c) We expected him here yesterday. He has not come till today. No one knows what happened to him. Perhaps he will reach here tomorrow. You will/may see him then.

EXERCISE 4

(i) We usually have dinner at about 10 pm.
I am having a birthday party on Friday. Are you free?

(ii) Biltu always does his homework as soon as he goes to school. Today he is doing his homework before going to school.

(iii) Dipika is seeing her brother off at the railway station this afternoon. Now I see what she means.

(iv) Tuhina has been thoroughly drenched. I think she is catching a cold. She catches cold in the rainy season.

(v) Bipin speaks Bengali well, but no Hindi. He is speaking to his friend. Let's wait for him.

EXERCISE 5

(a) After he has finished his hometask, he will go to play. When I have got my drawing coloured, it will look nice.

(b) I had shut the door before I got into bed.
The doctor came after the patient had died.
We had entered the room when it started to rain.

EXERCISE 6

(i) Passenger : Could you help me? I am going to Delhi tomorrow. Can you tell me when the Delhi Mail arrives ?
Booking Clerk : Let me see. You can get it early in the morning. It takes about eleven hours.
Passenger : What about the Rajdhani Express?
Booking Clerk : That's a faster train. You can save at least four hours of your time.
Passenger : Then I will not travel by Delhi Mail. I will travel by the Rajdhani Express.

(ii) Abdul : I don't feel quite well today.
Ayesha : Why don't you call in a doctor?
Abdul : No, I think I will be all right. Could you give me a cup of coffee please?
Ayesha : Certainly. Do you take sugar?
Abdul : Yes, one spoon.

(iii) Man : Look at this letter from the landlord. He will sell this house.
Wife : But what shall we do? We have nowhere to go. Where shall we find a place to live in?
Man : Don't worry. We will find a place. I have written to my friend. He will be able to help us.

EXERCISE 7

(i) Declarative mood, (ii) Declarative mood, (iii) Imperative mood, (iv) Imperative mood, (v) Imperative mood, (vi) Declarative mood, (vii) Imperative mood, (viii) Imperative mood, (ix) Imperative mood, (x) Subjunctive mood.

EXERCISE 8

Simple Present & Simple Past

We do the work.	We did the work.
Lila does the work.	Lila did the work.
He does the work.	He did the work.
She does the work.	She did the work.
They do the work.	They did the work.

Present Continuous & Past Continuous

We are doing the work.	We were doing the work.
You are doing the work.	You were doing the work.

Madhu is doing the work.	Madhu was doing the work.
Bina is doing the work.	Bina was doing the week.
He is doing the work.	He was doing the work.
She is doing the work.	She was doing the work.
They are doing the work.	They were doing the work.

Present Perfect & Past Perfect

We have done the work.	We had done the work.
You have done the work.	You had done the work.
Debu has done the work.	Debu had done the work.
Mini has done the work.	Mini had done the work.
He has done the work.	He had done the work.
She has done the work.	She had done the work.
They have done the work.	They had done the work.

Simple Future

I shall do the work.	Shila will do the work.
We shall do the work.	He will do the work.
You will do the work.	She will do the work.
Shibu will do the work.	They will do the work.

EXERCISE 9

Simple Present

Who teaches Economics?

What does Mr. Sen teach?

When does the sun shine?

When do you leave office?

Where do the US forces lead the men?

Present Continuous

What are you doing?

What are they doing?

Who is taking part in the game?

Who are talking to a number of people here?

What are the police doing?

Present Perfect

Who has complained about this problem?

Who has slipped in the bathroom and got his leg broken?

Who has broken the record of centuries in One-Day Match?

Where/Wherein have you found the letter?

Present Perfect Continuous

Who has been building the flyover for a few years?

How long has she been learning French?

How long has it been raining?

Simple Past

When did you receive this letter?

Who decided to continue the course?

Where did he learn Kannad?

How long did you stay with your grandparents?

Past Continuous

Who was shaking with anger (when he was punished)?

How long were the people working?

Who was reading a newspaper while his brother was watching TV?

Where was he working when I was living in Mumbai?

Past Perfect

Who found out that Sunita had lied to you?

Who had gone to bed when the phone rang?

Past Perfect Continuous

What had you been doing in the garden?

Who had been expecting the news for some time?

Simple Future

Where will you meet me?

When will he come back?

Future Continuous

Who will be delivering his lecture at the conference?

Who will be meeting us (you) shortly?

When will you be celebrating your sister's birthday?

Future Perfect

Will I have received the award by next year?

When will they have finished their task?

Future Perfect Continuous

What will you have been painting till Sunday morning?

How long will they have been working here?

EXERCISE 10

Simple Present

Yes, I do./No, I don't.

Yes, he reads newpaper./No, he does not read any newspaper.

Present Continuous

She is reading a novel, etc.

The boys are playing cricket in the field.

Present Perfect

Yes, he has attended the class./No, he has not attended the class.

Yes, the farmer has sown the seed in the field./No, the farmer has not sown the seed in the field.

Yes, the students have noticed my presence./No, the students have not noticed my presence.

Yes, I have seen it./No, I haven't seen it.

Present Perfect Continuous

I have been learning English for about a month, etc.

Yes, they have been putting a lot of money in Indian industry./No, they haven't been putting a lot of money in Indian industry.

Simple Past

I arrived here at 5 pm, etc.

Yes, I read the newspaper yesterday./No I didn't.

Past Continuous

Yes, he was driving his car very fast./No he was not driving his car very fast.

They were at home/in a hotel, etc.

Past Perfect

He had finished his work yesterday/a week ago, etc.

Yes, they had performed well in the competition./No, they hadn't.

Past Perfect Continuous

Our teachers had been planning a picnic for us.

I/We had been gossiping.

Simple Future

I'll answer (your questions).

I/We shall go to school.

Future Continuous

Mithun will be helping us to organise the party.

Future Perfect

Yes, I'll have finished my homework by the evening.

No, I won't have finished my homework by the evening.

They will have consulted their family physician tomorrow.

Future Perfect Continuous

I/We will have been enjoying our weekend.

CHAPTER 15 : VERBAL NOUN, GERUND AND PARTICIPLE

EXERCISE 1

(i) **doing**—Gerund, (ii) **playing**—Participle, (iii) **Coming**—Gerund, (iv) **playing**—Gerund, **studying**—Gerund, (v) **having**—Gerund, (vi) **playing**—Gerund, (vii) **being**—Participle, **beaten**—Participle, (viii) **Walking**—Gerund, (ix) **Hearing**—Participle, (x) **standing**—Participle, (xi) **hoarding**—Gerund, (xii) **reading**—Gerund, (xiii) **Praising**—Gerund, (xiv) **Jumping**—Gerund, (xv) **Asking, answering**—Gerund.

EXERCISE 2

(i) **approaching**—Present Participle, (ii) **Having**—Pr. Participle, (iii) **disgusted**—Past Participle, (iv) **pouring**—Pr. Participle, (v) **being**—Present Participle, (vi) **speaking**—Pr. Participle, (viii) **Seizing**—Pr. Participle.

EXERCISE 3

(i) Starting early, we arrived in time.
(ii) The gatekeeper having opened the gate, we entered.
(iii) We met a man carrying a basket.
(iv) Taking up a gun, the hunter went out to shoot the tiger.
(v) Having purchased the printed sari, the girl was charmed to see it.
(vi) Having resolved on a certain course, I acted with vigour.
(vii) Being delayed by a storm, the steamer came late.
(viii) I had troubles in making out the contents of the letter written badly.

EXERCISE 4

(i) As I heard the noise, I turned round.
(ii) We left the forest and advanced into the open path.
(iii) I walked up to the front door and rang the bell.
(iv) The robber mounted his horse and rode away.
(v) As he did not know the way, he asked a policeman.
(vi) While she was walking on the roof, she slipped and fell to the ground.
(vii) I once saw a girl who was walking on a tight rope.
(viii) As we had no guide with us, we lost our way.
(ix) As winter came on, the grasshopper had no food.
(x) He failed in the first attempt and made no further attempts.

EXERCISE 5

(a) **Present Participle :** A rolling stone, a running train, a blooming flower, boiling water.

Gerund as a Compound Noun

A dancing hall, a sleeping room, a travelling dress, a swimming costume.

(b) A rolling stone gathers no moss. Don't rouse a sleeping tiger. A blooming flower is beautiful to look at. Don't put your hand in boiling water.

(c) Primary education is the pressing need of our time. Hearing the noise, we rushed to the spot. She kept me waiting. Having rested a while, we continued our journey. The sun having risen, the fog dispersed. The fog having dispersed, the soldiers marched.

(d) A deserted house. A lost hope. A forsaken friend. Sunken cheeks.

(e) Deceived by his friends, he lost all hope.
Blinded by a dust storm, they lost their way.
Driven by hunger, he stole a piece of bread.
The frightened child began to cry.
The trees in the garden were laden with fruit.
It is widely circulated.

(f) Smoking is a bad habit. He gave up smoking. Swimming is a good exercise. He enjoyed swimming in the river. Sleeping is necessary to life. He is tired of sleeping over hours. One of his bad habits is smoking. He gave up the habit of smoking. He is fond of reading novels.

(g) Judgement delayed is judgement denied. He is addicted to the reading of thrillers.

CHAPTER 16 : MORE ABOUT ADVERBS AND ADVERBIALS

EXERCISE 1

There are Adverbs of three main types. They are :

(a) Simple Adverb, (b) Relative Adverb, (c) Interrogative Adverb.

Simple Adverb : The train arrived late. The news has been collected locally.

Relative Adverb : Show me the house where he was born. You may go where you like.

Interrogative Adverb : Where is Rohan? When did he come?

EXERCISE 2

- **easily**—Adverb modifying 'before'; **quickly**—Adverb modifying 'read'; **again**—Adverb modifying 'quarrel'; **carefully**—Adverb modifying 'looked'; **usually**—Adverb modifying 'looked'; **seldom**—Adverb modifying 'saw'; **almost**—Adverb modifying 'knew'; **out**—Adverb modifying 'go' away; **always**—Adverb modifying 'were'.

EXERCISE 3

(i) I have completely forgotten his name.

(ii) She was breathing heavily when she came on the fourth floor.

(iii) He faced the difficulties bravely.

(iv) The work has been perfectly done.

(v) Do not read so loudly.
(vi) I am eagerly waiting for you.
(vii) Probably his father will come here tomorrow.

EXERCISE 4

(i) Possibly he is ill.
(ii) Our team will surely win.
(iii) Certainly there won't be any difficulty.
(iv) Obviously my father will depend on me after his retirement.
(v) Unfortunately no one could escape from the burning hut.

EXERCISE 5

(i) The boy seldom stayed at school after the classes.
(ii) "It was mainly chance, young man", Davy said modestly.
(iii) Kajal pushed her quickly out of the room, and bolted the door from outside.
(iv) He prepared his lecture very carefully, but unfortunately could not deliver it.
(v) The missiles are being dangerously thrown and these are damaging the people in developed countries.

EXERCISE 6

(i) Most people know what is right and what is wrong. Unfortunately however, when the time for action comes, they often fail to act rightly. The trouble with them is that they are selfish and think only of themselves, not of others.
(ii) In the 21st century one of the greatest problems is pollution. In our cities, the air is constantly being polluted by smoke from factories and from carbon monoxide gases emitted by motor vehicles.
(iii) The warder who had fallen into the river was in a very critical situation, for he hardly knew how to swim. Every second that passed increased his danger of being snapped up by one of these voracious creatures. Suddenly one of the convicts, heeded by his nobler feelings, threw himself into the river.
(iv) Deaf education was first introduced in Germany in the 19th century, and it was not known well enough to many concerned parents.

CHAPTER 17 : MORE ABOUT PREPOSITIONS

EXERCISE 1

(a) on Sunday, (b) in January, (c) in 2008, (d) in Monday morning, (e) at noon, (f) at night, (g) at dawn, (h) in the morning, (i) in the afternoon, (j) at 10 'clock, (k) from dawn to dusk (l) between 2 pm and 4 pm.

EXERCISE 2

(a) Where do you come from?
(b) What are you afraid of?
(c) Please give him a chair to sit on.
(d) Please give a pen to write with.

EXERCISE 3

(i) He shouted at the top of his voice.
(ii) He got the prize by dint of hard work.
(iii) There is a tall tree in front of our school.
(iv) He told me this in course of conversation.
(v) The police arrived in the nick of time.
(vi) He did not go to school owing to/on account of his illness.
(vii) He started a business instead of crying for a job.
(viii) He did this with a view to helping his friend.
(ix) The bearer will receive the letter on behalf of me.
(x) He was given a farewell on the eve of his retirement.

CHAPTER 18 : APPROPRIATE PREPOSITIONS

EXERCISE 1

(a) He is absent from school.
(b) He was admitted to Class VI.
(c) This book belongs to him.
(d) Are you busy with your studies?
(e) Take care of your health.
(f) He will comply with my request.
(g) He has no control over his son.
(h) The man is eligible for the post.
(i) They will not be excused for coming late.
(j) She is familiar with my parents.
(k) He is not fit for the job.
(l) I am fond of sweets.
(m) I prefer sweets to meat.
(n) You can rely on him.
(o) He is senior to me.
(p) She is junior to him.
(q) This is superior to that.
(r) This is inferior to that.
(s) He is waiting for me.
(t) She waited on the patient.

EXERCISE 2

(a) Mr. John is a European. He deals in umbrella. But he deals well with the customers. He is aware of good relations with the customers. He has invited some of them to dinner today.

(b) Karim died of cholera. But his friend, Abdul died from over-eating though he wished to die for his country.

(c) The man is blind of one eye. But he is not blind to his son's faults. He knows very well that his son is lame of one leg. He is also hard of hearing. However, he devotes much time to study. He hoped that forture will smile on him. He is not ashamed of his physical deformity. He does not hanker after name or fame.

(d) I agree with you on this point. But I cannot agree to your previous proposal. However, you should not be angry with me for speaking against you. I am not at all angry at your conduct.

(e) He is fond of sweets. But I prefer fruit to sweets. In fact, fruit and honey are preferable to fish, or meat. But my friend differs with me on this point.

(f) You should abide by the rules of the school and you should not be absent from school. Your school is adjacent to your house and so you will not be excused for coming late.

(g) She is proud of her wealth. But you should not take pride in your health or wealth. You should not be devoid of common sense. Moreover, you should not laugh at the poor and you should have zeal for social work.

CHAPTER 19 : MORE ABOUT CONJUNCTIONS

EXERCISE 1

(1) and—joining 'you' and 'I' (pronoun to pronoun)
(2) or—joining two sentences 'was it true' and 'was it false'.
(3) but—joining 'poor' and 'honest in his dealings' (word to clause)
(4) If—joining 'you wish' and 'I will teach you to read' (sentence to sentence)
(5) but—joining 'I wish to read' and 'I dislike the trouble of reading' (sentence to sentence)
(6) how—joining 'Tell me' and 'I can learn…' (sentence to sentence)
(7) that—joining 'I can tell you' and 'nothing can be …' (sentence to sentence)
(8) till—joining 'you must go on working' and 'the sun goes down' (sentence to sentence)
(9) as soon as—joining 'the sun goes down' and 'you may stop work' (sentence to sentence)
(10) as—joining 'You should go home now' and 'the sun has set' (sentence to sentence)

(11) for—joining 'They wept' and 'they had lost their mother' (sentence to sentence)

(12) unless—joining 'you will miss the train' and 'you make haste' (sentence to sentence)

(13) whether—joining 'I have never heard' and 'you missed the first train' (sentence to sentence)

(14) lest—joining 'Do not get wet' and 'you should catch cold' (sentence to sentence)

(15) both... and—joining 'your' and 'your brother' (pronoun to noun)

(16) although—joining 'the sun is very hot today' and 'you may go out...',

provided—joining 'you may go out...' and 'you take...kind' (sentence to sentence).

and—joining 'you take an umbrella' and 'wear a hat of some kind' (clause to clause)

EXERCISE 2

(a) You must get up when the sun rises.
(b) You need not leave your bed till the sun rises.
(c) I could not find out where he lived.
(d) Wait here till I return.
(e) Take care lest you should fall.
(f) You are much more idle than you used to be.
(g) Many years have passed since I saw you last.
(h) I wish to know why you have been so lazy as before.
(i) Tell me if you can do it when the clock will strike nine.
(j) A man must do his best that/so that he may succeed.
(k) You should not despair if you have failed once.
(l) He who has failed once may succeed the second time, if he tries hard.
(m) You have neglected your work, and you know that you were doing wrong.
(n) I am afraid that he would not survive his illness.
(o) Either you or I must write that letter at once; as it must be sent within the next two hours.
(p) Gora sells both apples and oranges.
(q) Most insects have wings, but most ants do not.
(r) Who sweeps the rooms, washes the clothes and cooks the meals?
(s) Gahar is hard-working but he is not an intelligent boy.
(t) Hashina is thin and tall, but her brother is fat and short.
(u) Will you meet me at 4 pm or 4.30 pm?
(v) The girls are helping their mother and the boys are flying kites.
(w) If you keep on your habit, you may land up in jail.

CHAPTER 20 : ARTICLES AND DETERMINERS

EXERCISE 1

(a) a BDO, (b) an SDO, (c) a DM, (d) a BA, (e) an MA, (f) an FRCS, (g) a ewe, (h) a union, (i) a European, (j) an H.S. school, (k) a university, (l) an umbrella (m) a unique event, (n) a uniform speed, (o) a one-eyed man, (p) a one-act play, (q) an opinion, (r) a historical play (s) an honest man, (t) a High School

EXERCISE 2

It is a useful article. Animesh reads the Gita everyday. Gahar reads the Koran. This is a one-way road. Sri Lanka is an island. He is a Newton. He is the Newton of India. Bankimchandra is the Scott of Bengal. He is a BA, but his brother is an MA. It is a unanimous decision. He lives in the UK, but his sister lives in the USA. This is a High School, but that is an H.S. school.

EXERCISE 3

(i)	My father goes to (b)	(a)	school?
(ii)	Does your sister go to (a)	(b)	market.
(iii)	Tourists in Delhi go to see (h)	(c)	Park Street
(iv)	Tourists in Kolkata go to see (g)	(d)	Violin
(v)	Do you play (d)	(e)	Delhi
(vi)	The UBI is on (c)	(f)	Australia
(vii)	The smallest continent is (f)	(g)	Victoria Memorial
(viii)	His uncle lives in (e)	(h)	The Taj Mahal

EXERCISE 4

(i) Our house is nearest to their house.

(ii) A man is sitting on a branch of a tree.

(iii) At night we stayed at a hotel.

(iv) I am not satisfied with this book. Could you supply me another book?

(v) Is there any difference between the two?

(vi) The Aryans were very proud of their high birth. They were afraid of getting mixed up with the tribals. It was a false pride.å

EXERCISE 5

(i) Sarojini Naidu who was an Indian was born at Hyderabad in the Deccan, on the 13th February in 1879. Her father came of a Bengali family that was famous for learning, and she herself was a great scholar.

(ii) The Narmada is a name of a river in South India. It is an important river and is consideraed as a holy river in the South.

(iii) The gentleman walking with a stick in his hand is a very well-known person here.He is a professor in a university. He has just returned from the UK after a period of four years obtaining the Ph. D. from Oxford University.

EXERCISE 6

(i) "Is this the book you are telling me about"? "yes, It is on the life of ... . Satyajit Roy, one of the greatest sons of ... India.

(ii) Her sister is a musician. She plays ... sitar and ... . But her brother has no interest in ... music. He is a good sportsman. He plays ... football and ... hockey.

EXERCISE 7

(i) Do not look at me. Look above and see the moon and stars. There are unaccountable stars twinkling in the sky at night. In the morning they will disappear again.

(ii) One day an old man was walking on a road. He was carrying a bagful of sugar in his hand. That man was the secretary of a school. I knew him to be an honest person.

(iii) He saw a most wonderful sight. Through a little hole in the wall children had crept in, and they were sitting in branches of the trees. In every tree that he could see was a little child.

(iv) High above the city, on a tall column, stood the statue of the Happy Prince. He was gilded all over with thin leaves of fine gold, for eyes he had two bright sapphires, and a large red ruby glowed on his sword-hilt.

(v) The last one of this long procession of silent men and women was a little wizened old man. Even he carried a load of two baskets, slung on a pole on his shoulder, the same load of a folded quilt, a cauldron. Although the load was light, it was too much for the old man.

CHAPTER 21 : MODIFIERS

EXERCISE 1

(i) Don't try to get into a running train.

(ii) The farmers working in the field are very poor.

(iii) I found the girl standing at the door.

(iv) We saw a girl walking on the ropes.

(v) Only hard-working students will succeed.

(vi) Don't put your hand in boiling water.

EXERCISE 2

(i) A balanced diet is required for a growing baby.

(ii) Why have you such a worried look?

(iii) They took the wounded man to hospital.

(iv) You should learn spoken English too.

(v) Good books read in childhood are the real guides.

(vi) Don't sit on a broken chair.

(vii) A burnt child dreads the fire.

EXERCISE 3

(i) Look at the cows grazing in the field.

(ii) The girl came here dancing joyfully.

(iii) If she catches you reading her diary, she'll be furious.

(iv) The picture painted by the artist is wonderful.

(v) He advised me to apply for the vacated post.

(vi) He is busy writing (to write) some letters.

(vii) He fell down while boarding a bus.

(viii) We should avoid wastage of money.

CHAPTER 22 : STRUCTURAL AND NON-STRUCTURAL WORDS

EXERCISE 1

(i) That , (ii) of, (iii) and, (iv) the, (v) could, (vi) in, (vii) that, (viii) had, (ix) for, (x) then.

EXERCISE 2

(i) —(b), (ii) —(d), (iii) —(a), (iv) —(c)

EXERCISE 3

(i) for, (ii) a, (iii) the

EXERCISE 4

(i) with, (ii) to, (iii) a

EXERCISE 5

(i) with, (ii) about, (iii) with, (iv) a

EXERCISE 6

Mr Smith is a European. He deals in umbrella, but he deals with the customers very well. All Europeans are not the same.

CHAPTER 23 : NARRATION/REPORTING

EXERCISE 1

(1) The teacher told the boy that he had forgotten the lesson.

(2) The boy said that he would go out and play.

(3) He said that he was happy to be there that day.

(4) They said that they would play the game again (the) next day.

(5) The boy said that two and two make four. [not, made]

(6) She told them that she had lost her books and theirs too.

(7) The princess says that she has lost her way.

(8) They say that they must keep their locality clean.

(9) The girl says that these books are theirs, but this one is hers.

(10) The Happy Prince said that he had led the dance in the great hall.

EXERCISE 2

A. (1) The boy asked me if I would accompany him.

(2) She asked me if she would post those letters for me.

(3) He asked me if I had done my hometask.

(4) Rahim asked if it was good or bad.

(5) The traveller asked if there was anybody there.

(6) He asked me if I was going with him.

(7) Hasina asked the man if he knew Mr. Ali.

(8) The man asked me if I knew where he lived.

(9) She asked me if I had written to her before.

(10) Lila asked me if I could tell her his address.

B. (1) He wanted to know which animal I was going to kill.

(2) Edison asked John what he had thought of it.

(3) I asked them who they were and what they wanted of us.

(4) I asked her where she had been yesterday.

(5) Father asked me when I had done it.

(6) I asked George which pen he was using.

(7) Mother asked the boy what his father was.

(8) They asked him which fish he had caught.

(9) He asked how such a man could be a teacher.

(10) I asked him why he had failed.

(11) He asked me when the Down train would arrive.

(12) The examiner asked who was the first man to land on the moon.

C. (1) I asked him if he was going home and assumed that he was going.

(2) He asked me if I had done my hometask and assumed that I had not.

(3) Father asked me if I had bought a pen from market for him and assumed that I had.

(4) My friend asked me if I has read the Ramayana and assumed that I had not.

(5) Mr. Kamat asked if they had performed the job well and assumed that they had not.

EXERCISE 3

A. (1) The master ordered his servant to do as he had told him.
(2) The teacher asked (ordered) the boys not to make so much noise.
(3) Kanika requested me to lend her my pen.
(4) He pleaded to be quiet and listen to his words.
(5) She requested her father to excuse her that time.
(6) The general ordered his soldiers to march forward.

B. (1) I requested the teacher that I might be allowed to come in.
(2) He proposed (suggested) that they should wait for the award.
(3) I said he might (might be allowed to) do what he liked.
(4) Father told his son that he must do that.
(5) The hare proposed to the tortoise that they should run a race.
(6) Rekha urged her mother to let her look out of the window.

EXERCISE 4

(1) I wished that he might live long.
(2) Nilima wished that I might recover soon.
(3) Mother prayed that God might grant him a long life.
(4) The holy man prayed for prevailing peace.
[Or] The holy man prayed that peace might prevail.
(5) She wished that his/her son might recover from illness soon.
(6) He wished that he could bring his departed friend back to life.

EXERCISE 5

(1) He exclaimed in grief that the war had killed all his family.
(2) He exclaimed in joy that his friend had come.
(3) The teacher expressed his disgust and said that he was a liar.
(4) They applauded by saying that it was a capital hit.
(5) The girl exclaimed in joy that she was happy then.
(6) Addressing his men as comrades the leader bade goodbye to them.
(7) He exclaimed that he had been very selfish.
(8) The girl exclaimed in wonder that it was a very fine picture.
(9) The teacher exclaimed in disgust that he was a very stupid fellow.
(10) Tom exclaimed that John was very clever.
(11) They exclaimed in wonder that it was a very interesting piece of painting.
(12) He exclaimed (swore) by the name of Heaven (God) that he would never steal again.

EXERCISE 6

A. 1.

(i) [Reporting on behalf of Corrie]

I begged Charlotte's pardon and said that I ought not to have talked about the war to her—especially that day. Mrs Meldon told me [Corrie and Henry being the same person] that she did not mind and added that the War Office was not the war after all.

(ii) [Reporting on behalf of Mrs Meldon]

Corrie begged pardon of me [Charlotte and Mrs Meldon being the same person] and said that he ought not to have talked about the war to me—especially that day. I told him that I did not mind and also said that the War Office was not the war after all.

(iii) [Reporting on behalf of a third person]

Corrie begged Charlotte's pardon and said that he ought not to have talked about the war to her—especially that day. Mrs Meldon said that she did not mind and added that the War Office was not the war after all.

2. Corrie asked Mrs Meldon what the hell she was doing. Mrs Meldon replied that she was destroying his foul invention. (Laughing harshly) Corrie said that won't destroy it, as he had got it in his head. And all that she (Charlotte) had done was to make a mess on his floor.

3. Davy put his hand out to Mr. Faraday.

   Jumping to his feet Michael Faraday responded respectfully.

   Davy said (proposed) that they should sit down there and talk the matter over.

4. Father asked Schatz how he was feeling.

   Schatz replied that it was just the same, so far. Father asked Schatz why he didn't try to sleep. He added that he (father) would wake him (Schatz) up for the medicine.

5. Schatz asked his father about how long it would be before he died.

   Father told him that he was not going to die. And being astonished a little he (father) asked him (Schatz) what was the matter with him.

   Schatz replied that he was sure to die. He had heard him say a hundred and two.

   Father told him that people wouldn't die with a fever of one hundred and two. And he added that it was a silly way to talk.

6. Gandhi asked Fischer if he didn't like vegetables. Fischer said (replied) that he didn't like the taste of those vegetables three days running.

   Gandhi advised him that he must add plenty of salt and lemon.

   Fischer asked Gandhi if he (Gandhi) wanted him (Fischer) to kill the taste.

   Gandhi laughingly said that it won't kill the taste, rather it would enrich the taste. Fischer said jokingly that he (Gandhi) was so non-violent he (Gandhi) wouldn't even kill a taste.

7. Addressing dearly Mrs Meldon as Charlotte, Corrie begged her pardon as he did not meet her at the station.

Addressing Corrie as Henry, Mrs Meldon said that it didn't matter. She added that only she thought he was coming, and haltingly repeated that she thought he would come and she waited a long time in the cold.

8. Addressing respectfully as Sir, Hannah told Corrie that Mrs Meldon was not very happy that day.

   Being astonished, Corrie asked Hannah why Mrs Meldon was not happy.

   And he added with assertion that he was happy.

   Hannah informed him that it was three years back that day since her son was killed in the war.

9. Corrie told Mrs Meldon that he was going to make war horrible, really horrible.

   Mrs Meldon responded affirmatively.

   Corrie told Charlotte that he had got something there, the formula for a bomb that would make war not only stupendously horrible, but would end it almost as quickly as it began.

   Mrs Meldon enquired if it was on that table.

   Corrie admitted it.

10. A passenger asked the booking clerk for four tickets to Panaji.

    The booking clerk wanted to know what Class.

    The passenger said that he wanted Second Class. The booking clerk wanted to know if he would like to have First Class tickets for the sea part of the journey from Nagar Haveli.

    The passenger wanted to know what would be the difference in price between the two Classes per ticket.

    The booking clerk said that it would be some twentyfive rupees, and it was not too much. But it would make his journey extremely enjoyable.

11. Son asked his father if (whether) they should take a taxi or a bus to go to the exhibition.

    Father said that it would be better they should take a bus. It was really difficult getting a taxi at that rush hour.

    Son asked his father if they should go to the next bus stop. That was the terminus. There they would get vacant seats.
    Father took it as a good idea.

12. Mr. Holmes greeted the madam and introduced himself as Sherlock Holmes. And pointing out to Watson he introduced his friend Dr. Watson. He added that before him she could speak freely. But first he would like to order a cup of hot tea, for he saw that she was shivering.

    The lady said (in a low voice) that it was not cold which made her shiver.

    Mr. Holmes asked her what was it then.
    The lady told him that it was fear and terror.

B.1. [In a crowded bus]

You : Excuse me. I stepped on your foot accidentally.

Somebody : That doesn't matter.

[Reporting]

In a crowded bus I accidentally stepped on somebody's foot. I begged his pardon and he said he did not mind.

2. [At a railway station]

You : Excuse me. Could you give me a change for a fifty-rupee note?

Somebody : Sorry. I can't/No problem. Here it is.

[Reporting]

At a railway station I wanted to have a cup of tea, but I had only a fifty-rupee note. I asked somebody there for giving me a change. I asked him if he could give me a change. He expressed his regret./He offered it readily.

3. [At the neighbour's door]

You : If you don't mind could you tone down your radio? It's too loud and I feel disturbed.

Neighbour : Sorry! I'll do it now.

[Reporting]

My neighbour's radio was too loud and I knocked at his door. I politely asked him to tone down his radio, as I felt disturbed. My neighbour begged my pardon and told me that he would do it instantly.

4. [In a town]

The stranger : Excuse me. Could you tell me the way to the post office?

You : Go ahead. Turn left at the next crossing and you'll find the post office on the left side.

[Reporting]

In our town a stranger met me and asked the way to the post office. I told him to go ahead and turn left at the next crossing, and then he would find the post office on the left side.

5. [In a town]

You : Hello/Hi Rupam ! Where have you been? I haven't seen you for two years. Please come to our home and spend the weekend with us.

Your friend : Nice to meet you. I was in Japan for two years and have come here only the other day. Be sure I'll join you at your home at the weekend. Thanks a lot.

[Reporting]

An old friend of mine had come to our town and I met him on the road. I asked him where he had been for two years. I invited him to come and spend the weekend with us. My friend responded courteously and told me that he was in Japan for two years. He added that he had come to our town only the other day. He assured me that he would join us at our home at the weekend. He also thanked me a lot.

C. [Reporting a telephone talk]

The PA said 'hello' over telephone.

Mr. Roy greeted him and asked him if he could speak to Mr. Sen.

The PA told him that he (Mr Sen) had not yet returned from Mumbai and added that possibly he would be there (at his office) that night.

Mr. Roy said that he had telephoned at his (Mr Sen's) home that morning, but couldn't get him. He requested the PA to give Mr Sen a message from him. It was about their meeting on Friday. He also said that he had been suddenly called from the Head office. And so it was better to postpone their meeting until next week.

The PA assured him and Mr. Roy thanked him.

[Reporting on behalf of the PA]

Mr. Roy rang up to speak to you. He telephoned at your home too, but couldn't get you. He informed that he had been suddenly called from the Head office and it was better to postpone your meeting until next week.

CHAPTER 24 : VOICE CHANGE/DESCRIBING A PROCESS

EXERCISE 1

Tenses	Voice	Indefinite	Continuous	Perfect
Present	Active	I eat rice.	I am eating rice.	I have eaten rice.
	Passive	Rice is eaten by me.	Rice is being eaten by me.	Rice has been eaten by me.
Past	Active	I ate rice.	I was eating rice.	I have eaten rice.
	Passive	Rice was eaten by me.	Rice was being eaten by me.	Rice had been eaten by me.
Future	Active	I shall eat rice.	I shall be eating rice.	I shall have eaten rice.
	Passive	Rice will be eaten by me.	—	Rice will have been eaten by me.

EXERCISE 2

Penicillin was invented by a scientist in 1928.

This school was built in 1990.

A letter was written to you by me.

A song will be sung by Sumita.

A picture is being drawn by Rakesh.

A flower was being plucked by the girl.

The book has been read by him.

The garden has been forgotten by Spring.

A rupee will be given me by him.
[or] I shall be given a rupee by him.
The boy will be punished by the Headmaster.
A good fight was fought by them.
His bag had been stolen by the thief.
The children were often looked well by mother.
Your parents should be obeyed (by you).
English is taught us by the Headmaster.
[or] We are taught English by the Headmaster.
You are requested to do this work.
Promises must be kept.
What cannot be cured must be endured.
By whom has this been done?
Why he has done this [Why this has been done by him] is not known to me.
Was any defect pointed out by you?
Be prepared for the worst.
Has your question been answered by anyone?
Can you ever be forgotten by me?
How many guests were invited (by you)?
It is now time for the names to be called over.
That it was done by him is known to me.
[or] It is known to me that it was done by him.
Let not the lame man be laughed at.
Let not the poor be looked down upon.
I was compelled to go there.
Reference books should not be taken out of the library.
Your keys were found on the top of the almirah.
The rate of taxation has been increased to thirty percent.
He was elected President (by them).

EXERCISE 3

Please do this.
They elected him President.
Mr Sen presided over the meeting.
Do this work.
Please put off your shoes.
Do you see the moon?
The mason has repaired the house.
They speak English.
You must do your duty.

We should love all the children.

What does he see?

I have lost my pen.

He dreamt a dream.

The police has caught the thief.

They will take over the charge tomorrow.

We know that the earth is round.

EXERCISE 4

(a) They cut grain stalks and tie them in bundles.
They thresh stalks to separate grain from stalk.
They store grain in a grannery.

(b) Smoke constantly pollutes the air. Rotten rubbish pollutes the ground. Chemicals and other wastes from factories also pollute water.

EXERCISE 5

Leaves of tea plant are plucked and then taken to the factory. There they are weighed and prepared. First the leaves are spread on flat trays. These trays are then taken to a heated room and kept there for about twenty hours. The heat softens the leaves. Next the leaves are passed through a machine which curls and crushes the leaves. Then they are placed in drawers and kept there in layers of one or two inches thick. The drawers thereafter are covered with damp curtains. Here the leaves change their colour and look like bright copper. They also get their fine flavour here. Thus tea is prepared for marketing.

EXERCISE 6

The preparation of edible oil from mustard seeds goes through a number of steps.

First mustard seeds are collected and dried. After that the dried seeds are put into the hawler. Then a little water is added to it for extracting oil. Thereafter oil cakes are separated. Next, oil is collected in containers and sealed. Now oil is ready for use.

EXERCISE 7

Drinking water from Palta Water Works is supplied to Kolkata through a number of steps.

First, raw Ganga water is extracted. Then it is purified by mixing alum. After that it is reserved in a big tank. Then it is filtered in filter beds. Thereafter chlorine is charged and super-purification is done in filter houses. After testing it, it is taken into pressure house. From there the drinking water is delivered (supplied) to Kolkata.

EXERCISE 8

Milk is collected and sent to factory. There it is weighed and tested. Then cream is separated through a special process. Now it is heated at 72°C. After that it is cooled. Finally it is packed or bottled for delivery.

CHAPTER 25 : PHRASES

EXERCISE 1

(i) to win the first prize, (ii) To win a prize, (iii) getting people into trouble, (iv) having to punish his friends, (v) her birthday party, (vi) all her friends, (vii) to answer the question, (viii) stealing the money, (ix) To write such rubbish, (x) Thinking good thoughts, (xi) Travelling in a crowdy train, the present condition of the railway system, (xii) Standing about in cold wind.

EXERCISE 2

(i) I do not expect such a situation.
(ii) I don't intend to go there.
(iii) My father hates all sorts of lying.
(iv) My brother loves all kinds of fast food.
(v) Her sudden appearance surprised my mother.
(vi) Singing in a loud voice gives me no pleasure.
(vii) To do this task is not so easy.
(viii) His sister promised neither to be too stupid nor to be too smart.
(ix) Such a shabby dress is disgraceful.
(x) The poor debtor intended to pay back his debt.

EXERCISE 3

(i) built of stone, (ii) with a kindly nature, (iii) of very considerable renown, (iv) made of saffron silk, (v) of great versatility, (vi) with a bad temper, (vii) with plenty of impudence, (viii) without a friend, (ix) stained with blood, (x) covered with mud.

EXERCISE 4

(i) Mr Birla is a wealthy man.
(ii) None should throw stones, who lives in a glass-house.
(iii) I like to see a smiling face.
(iv) A caged wild beast is a sorry sight.
(v) He is a friendless man.
(vi) I met a little cottage girl.
(vii) She was a great promising girl.
(viii) The boys bore a peculiar banner.
(ix) In a low voice he told the adventurous tale.

EXERCISE 5

(i) A meadow full of grass stretched before us.
(ii) I have passed night without sleep.
(iii) He is a cricketer by profession.
(iv) Mr Varma is a man of wealth.
(v) Do you know which day is longer than any other day in a year?

(vi) The poor beggar dwelt in a hut made of wood.
(vii) How did he get such a thing of value?
(viii) Lalu prefers a pot of earth for taking tea.
(ix) Netaji Subhas Chandra Bose is a person without fear.
(x) I admit that he is a man of sense.

EXERCISE 6

(i) under a great banyan tree, (ii) in the middle of a forest, (iii) to the last, (iv) in proper colours, (v) with a loud sound, (vi) at the top of his voice, (viii) with all his might, (viii) at any cost, (ix) on the pulse of the nation, (x) on her face.

EXERCISE 7

(i) Horses run fast/speedily.
(ii) You can buy it everywhere.
(iii) Go there and pay your fees.
(iv) Stop writing now.
(v) Then the queen arrived.
(vi) These posts are held unreserved.
(vii) He has proved his fitness satisfactorily.
(viii) I hope that you will come soon.
(ix) This picture has not been painted properly.
(x) He earns his living honestly.
(xi) He shouted loudly.
(xii) It has been done unwisely.

EXERCISE 8

(i) Do your homework with care.
(ii) The bodies in the ill-fated bus were mangled in a terrible way.
(iii) In the afternoon the wind blew in a violent manner.
(iv) In former times he worked in a private company.
(v) The news has come to us at a recent date.
(vi) He expects to get promotion at an early date.
(vii) The children are playing with cheers.
(viii) The soldiers fought for the country in a brave manner.
(ix) She binds her hair in a beautiful style.
(x) He is preparing his best to go to a foreign country.
(xi) He seems to have acted in a proper way.

EXERCISE 9

(i) on this spot—Adverbial phrase
(ii) at that moment—Adverbial phrase
(iii) on the island—Adjective phrase

(iv) at an early date—Adverbial phrase
(v) from this very moment—Adverbial phrase
(vi) to Bangalore—Adjective phrase
(vii) in a loud voice—Adverbial phrase
(viii) like a born orator—Adverbial phrase
(ix) such treatment at your hands—Noun phrase
(x) in spite of—Prepositional phrase.

EXERCISE 10

(i) Hearing the noise—Participial phrase formed by a Present Participle
(ii) Seeing him fall from the free—Participial phrase formed by a Past Participle
(iii) Loudly knocking at the gate—Participial phrase formed by a Present Participle
(iv) Deceived by his friends—Participial phrase formed by a Past Participle
(v) Blinded by a dust-storm—Participial phrase formed by a Past Participle
(vi) Sitting on the gate—Participial phrase formed by a Present Participle
(vii) Entering the room—Participial phrase formed by a Present Participle
(viii) Walking in the field—Participial phrase formed by a Present Participle
(ix) Frankly speaking—Participial phrase formed by a Present Participle
(x) Considering his abilities—Participial phrase formed by a Present Partciple
(xi) Having rested a while—Participial phrase formed by a Perfect Participle

EXERCISE 11

(i) a good player—Phrase in apposition
(ii) The dinner being over—Absolute phrase
(iii) a Punjabi poet—Phrase in apposition
(iv) the city of temples—Phrase in apposition
(v) Frankly speaking—Perenthetical phrase
(vi) It being a very hot day—Absolute phrase
(vii) to speak the truth—Perenthetical phrase
(viii) the great emperor—Phrase in apposition

EXERCISE 12

(i) The boy wants to eat something.
(ii) He is too weak to walk.
(iii) He has two sons to teach.
(iv) He has a cycle to sell.
(v) She works hard to pass the examination.
(vi) Early to bed is a good exercise to follow.
(vii) Do you enjoy swimming as a good exercise?
(viii) We enjoy playing cricket.

EXERCISE 13

(i) Being tired, he rested for a while.

(ii) Seeing me come, he ran away.

(iii) The workers belong to a tribe dwelling in the hills.

(iv) This is an axe made of iron.

(v) A bird in the hand is worth two in the bush.

(vi) He told a tale about his cruel deeds.

(vii) He tells a tale with a ring of truth in it.

(viii) Here is a boy of great promise.

(ix) He wore a turban made of silk.

(x) He has done a deed of shame.

EXERCISE 14

(i) The train was late in the usual way.

(ii) She spoke the truth without any fear.

(iii) He fought alone without any help.

(iv) He returned home in the evening.

(v) The dead bodies were mangled in a terrible manner.

(vi) Let us cease work from the very moment.

(vii) They succeeded in the long run.

(viii) The wind blew with great violence.

(ix) He has proved his case to my satisfaction.

(x) He may come at an early date.

EXERCISE 15

(i) He won the prize by dint of hard work.

(ii) He got the award by means of hard labour.

(iii) He succeeded at last by virtue of continuous labour.

(iv) He sacrificed his life for the sake of his country.

(v) Call the Fire Brigade in case of fire.

(vi) He told me this in course of conversation.

(vii) He is waiting in front of the school.

(viii) They went to the jungle in search of a deer.

(ix) In spite of his proverty, he donated a considerable amount in the fund for the flood-stricken people.

(x) The Headmaster welcomed the visitors on behalf of the school.

EXERCISE 16

(i) Alexander, a powerful king, invaded India.

(ii) Ashoka, a great king, loved his people dearly.

(iii) Akbar, the greatest Mughal emperor, was secular among the Muslim rulers.

(iv) Kalidas wrote 'Shakuntala', a play in Sanskrit.

(v) Bishnupur, a town of temples, is situated in West Bengal.

EXERCISE 17

(i) The sun having risen, the fog dispursed.

[Or] Having the sun risen, the fog dispersed.

(ii) Having the fog dispersed, the soldiers began to march.

(iii) Having the rain fallen, the crops revived.

(iv) The sun having set, we returned to our house.

(v) The war having broken out, the prices rose high.

(vi) The bell having rung, the students entered their class.

(vii) The treaty having failed, the war broke out.

(viii) It being very hot, we could not get out of home.

(ix) It being a holiday, we went out for a picnic.

(x) Having the loadshedding occurred frequently, business is suffering.

CHAPTER 26 : SENTENCES AND ITS CLAUSES/ JOINING/SPLITTING

EXERCISE 1

1. A Simple sentence is one that contains only one subject and one finite verb.
   Examples :
   Rakesh is an employee in the State Bank.
   He works there from 10 am to 4 pm.
2. A Complex sentence is one that contains one principal clause and one or more subordinate clause or clauses.
   Examples :
   I know that he is very intelligent.
   This is the boy who is very intelligent.
   You may go where you like.
3. A Compound sentence is one that contains two or more independent clauses or coordinating clauses.
   Examples :
   Puja is a good girl and she loves her brother.
   You may stay here or leave the place.
   He tried hard but failed at last.

4. A Principal clause is an independent clause and a Subordinate Clause depends on a Principal clause.

5. Coordinating Clauses are independent clauses joined by conjunctions for coordination.

6. There are three types of Subordinate Clauses. They are—(i) Noun Clause or Nominal Clause, (ii) Adjective Clause or Relative Clause and (iii) Adverbial Clause.

   Noun Clause : He said that he would go home.

   Adjective Clause : The boy who came here is my friend.

   Adverbial Clause : I shall go out to play when I finish my hometask.

7.

Sentence	Classification of sentences with clauses
If you speak, you will die.	This is a complex sentence (a) You will die—Pr. cl. (b) if you speak—sub. Adv. cl.
I know that he is honest.	This is a Complex sentence. (a) I know—Pr. cl. (b) That he is honest—Sub. N. cl.
He is honest though he is poor.	This is a Complex sentence. (a) He is honest—Pr. cl. (b) though he is poor—Sub. Adv. cl.
He is poor but he is honest.	This is a Compound sentence. (a) He is poor—Pr. cl. (b) He is honest—Sub. N. cl. Conjunction—but
She must weep or she will die.	This is a Compound sentence. (a) She must weep—Coord. cl. (b) she will die—Coord. cl. Conjunction—or.
He came home and began to work.	This is a Compound sentence. (a) He came home—Coord. cl. (b) he began to work—Coord. cl. Conjunction—and
He was the last man who went there.	This is a Complex sentence. (a) He was the last man—Pr. cl. (b) who went there—Sub. Adj. cl.
When he reached the station, he saw that the train had started.	This is a Complex sentence. (a) He saw—Pr. cl.

	(b) that the train had started—Sub. N. cl. (c) When he reached the station—. Sub. Adv. cl.
He not only caned the boy but also fined him.	This is a Compound sentence. (a) He caned the boy—Coord. cl. (b) he fined him—Coord. cl. Conjunction—not only…but also

EXERCISE 8

(a) Do you know where he was born?
(b) He told me that he had passed the examination.
(c) I am sure that you had made no mistake.
(d) I know that it will rain.
(e) We know that she is an intelligent girl.
(f) Nobody knows why Harish was weeping.

EXERCISE 9

(a) She told me the address which I wrote on a piece of paper.
(b) The man who answered the phone told me that you were out.
(c) I saw a car which was rushing past the park.
(d) He is a soldier who must show discipline.
(e) Do you know the place where Vidyasagar was born?
(f) Here is the pencil that you lost yesterday.
(g) Listen to those things that teachers say.
(h) The man whom you saw the other day is Mr. Bose's nephew.
(i) Romario, who was in the Brazil team, got the Gold Football Award.
(j) He gave me his test books which did me much good.
(k) The girl who is a good basketball player is a friend of mine.
(l) Mr Kapoor whom you saw yesterday is my uncle.
(m) The boy who came to me yesterday is my classmate.
(n) Those frogs who can fly, generally live in trees.
(o) The swallow who was going to die bade goodbye to the Happy Prince.
(p) I am familiar with the boy of Class IX who bagged many prizes on the day of the prize-giving ceremony.

EXERCISE 10

(a) Garbage is dangerous to human health if it remains uncollected for a long period.
(b) The odour specialists have been unable to identify any primary smell although much work has been done in the field.

(c) Walter was ready to stand under the tree because he wanted to save his father.

(d) He cannot buy his books because he is poor.

(e) As soon as I entered the room, I felt something was wrong.

(f) The plant stopped feeding when it was shaded.

(g) He finished his work when the clock struck five.

(h) I shall not go out unless you come.

(i) Although (Though) he has been running a high temperature, he wishes to go to school.

(j) He jumped out of bed when the bell rang.

(k) I cannot compete with you as (because) you are stronger.

(l) I left the meeting because there was an awful noise.

[or] I left the meeting where there was awful noise.

(m) He learnt the fact when he was angry with himself.

(n) Although (Though) you are powerful, I am not afraid of you.

(o) He stared at me long as he seemed never to have seen me before.

EXERCISE 11

(a) Sharmila as well as Ayesha is a student of this school.

[or] Sharmila and Ayesha are the students of this school.

[or] Both Sharmila and Ayesha are the students of this school.

[or] Not only Sharmila but also Ayesha are the students of this school.

(b) Rahaman is not a good student, but he is a good player.

(c) You may accept the offer or refuse it.

[or] You may either accept the offer or refuse it.

(d) Neither I nor my brother knew anything of it.

(e) You must pay the price or you must return the goods.

(f) The gardener was old, yet he planted some mango trees in my uncle's garden.

(g) Rabin was my sincere friend and he desired to help me in my difficulties.

(h) The Headmaster not only thanked me, but also rewarded me.

(i) He is both dishonest and wicked to the backbone.

[or] He is not only dishonnest, but also wicked to the backbone.

EXERCISE 12

(a) Seeing me come, he ran away.

(b) Being tired, he took rest for a while.

(c) Entering the room, a thief had found the room empty.

(d) Being angry with me, he did not speak to me.

(e) Addressing the meeting, the Prime Minister asked for everybody's cooperation.

(f) Having lost his way, he wandered about from place to place.

(g) I saw a wounded tiger.

(h) Determined to oppose the bill, he stood up to speak.

(i) He has many sons to educate them.

(j) He has a car to sell.

(k) I have many friends here to stand by me.

(l) I went there to help him.

(m) He has a large family to maintain.

(n) He is too weak to walk.

(o) I am determined not to do it again.

EXERCISE 13

(a) I saw the injured boy.

(b) The stolen watch was recovered at last.

(c) Being absorbed in deep thought the boy could not answer my question.

(d) Hearing the sound they sprang up.

(e) His misery is too great to bear it.

(f) He has a house to let.

EXERCISE 14

(a) Hearing my illness, he at once went to the doctor without waiting for me.

(b) It was not difficult for the healthy and strong boy to lift the load of forty kilograms.

(c) I am sorry as you were absent from the meeting in the Town Hall.

(d) I heard a loud noise like the bursting of a bomb that came from a house close by.

(e) A fire broke out in the multi-storeyed building at Burrabazar at midnight on Sundry last.

(f) I saw a poor old man bent down with age on my way to school.

(g) An atom bomb that was dropped on Hiroshima, a city of Japan, destroyed it.

(h) He keeps some well-trained dogs to guard his house.

(i) As the sky is cloudy, it will be better for him to take an umbrella.

(j) The new book given by my father teaches me grammar.

EXERCISE 15

(a) You deserved to pass. I think so. You have failed. I am sorry to hear this.

(b) He was speaking. The prince had suddenly died. A man entered. He told him this.

(c) He was a poor man. He had found a bag full of one lakh rupees. He said nothing of it. He left the country.

(d) A boy came to me for help. He is a liar. He is also a cheat. Everybody knows it.

(e) The old man was once very rich. He was now deserted by all. He was lying in sick-bed in his lonely hut. I could not but feel sorry for him.

(f) It is the duty of every man to love his neighbours. It is also the duty to help them to the best of his power. He taught us this.

(g) I was in my native village during the summer vacation. I often went to the houses of the poor people. I went there to know their difficulties.

(h) He was ill with fever. He was not able to accompany me. I heard this. I gave up the idea of going to Darjeeling.

(i) We heard the cry. We rushed to the spot to help the passengers. They were trapped in the bus. The bus was overturned.

(j) He found my purse. He returned it to me. He did not take anything from it. I gave him my thanks.

(k) I could not carry out his orders. I did not inform him of my inability in time. So he was displeased with me.

(l) The evening mist rose. He came to the cave. He drew breath. He looked down the valley.

(m) He went to Darjeeling. His sister also went there. I often met them at the Mall. We walked together.

(n) I was young. You were old. You were experienced too. I was afraid of your age and dignity. I kept silent before you.

(o) I lost my way. I asked a policeman to direct me. He was new to his work. He could not help me.

(p) Homer was a great poet. He was born somewhere. Nobody knows the place of his birth.

(q) A drowning man shouted for help. A sailor heard it. He plunged into the river to save the man's life.

(r) You are still immature. You felt elated at the praise of others. Such reaction of yours is impractical.

(s) We waste our energies too often over trifles. We all make this mistake.

(t) India had no culture, or next to none. We take it for granted. It is for the want of opportunity in our course of study.

(u) That unfortunate boy lived at the confluence of the Ganges and Jamuna. What river had he seen? He was asked (this question). He had not seen any. He replied thus.

(v) The Hindu Code Law was duly passed. It did not provide beleaguered women respite from violence. Such violence gripped their lives.

(w) The law was being hotly debated. We too arranged many meetings and gatherings among women. We collected many signatures in its support.

(x) Johnny crashed through the garden gate. He stormed down the path. He demolished some of his father's prize blooms with his trailing satchel.

(y) In urban areas a minority of car owners cause massive pollution. They cause congestion, noise and accidents too. It may be taken for instance. All these are at the expense of the public at large.

(z) There are present trends of rapid ground water tables in large parts of the country. They are utterly unsustainable. They call for urgent attention.

CHAPTER 27 : TRANSFORMATION OF SENTENCES

EXERCISE 1

1. Who can bear an unprovoked insult?
2. Who ever saw a brighter daybreak than this?
3. We laugh if you tickle us.
4. Everybody wishes to be happy.
5. I shall not forget those happy days.
6. That is not the way a gentleman should behave.
7. This is not the suitable dress to wear in school.
8. Nobody can trust such a liar.
9. Was he not a fool to act thus?
10. There is no use of such an old thing.
11. Everybody knows him.
12. None (Nobody) can touch pitch without being defiled.

EXERCISE 2

1. There was a very beautiful sight.
2. Man is a very wonderful piece of work.
3. He manages his bat very awkwardly.
4. These mangoes have very delicious flavour.
5. I wish (that) I were there at that time.
6. How clever he is!
7. How beautiful it is to look at!
8. What a fall you have!

EXERCISE 3

1. I was not sure whether it was you.
2. Only a coward flees from his duty.
3. Learned men are sometimes judicious.
4. Great men are of various nations and classes.
5. No sooner did he come (had he come), he made objections.
6. He is not always foolish.
7. No man never mistakes.
8. I do not care what he says about me.
9. Everybody doubts his honesty.
10. Where there is smoke, there is fire.
11. He will never see his home again.

EXERCISE 4

1. She is not more intelligent than her brother.
2. No other girl in her class is as good as she.
   [Or] She is better than any other girl in her class.

3. Gold is more precious than most other metals.
   [Or] Very few metals are as precious as gold.
4. No other animal is as useful as the cow.
   [Or] The cow is more useful than all other animals.
5. Mumbai is richer than most other cities in India.
   [Or] Very few cities in India are as rich as Mumbai.
6. No other girl in the class is as good as Saraswati.
   [Or] Saraswati is the best girl in the class.
7. Akbar was greater than most other emperors of India.
   [Or] Very few emperors of India was as great as Akbar.
8. The Rajdhani Express runs fastest.
   [Or] No other train runs as fast as the Rajdhani Express.
9. Wealth is not as valuable as health.
10. America is one of the richest countries.
    [Or] America is richer than most other countries.

EXERCISE 5

1. He is so proud that he cannot beg.
2. It is never so late that it cannot be mended.
3. She was so late that she could not hear the first speech.
4. The boy is so old that he cannot be whipped.
5. He speaks so fast that he (his speech) cannot be understood.
6. The fact is too evident to require a proof.
7. Be not so eager for praise.
8. The sun is too hot for us to go out at present.
9. Many more cooks than required spoil the broth.
10. He reached the station so late that he could not catch the train.

EXERCISE 6

1. The news that he has succeeded has been published in the newspaper.
2. If he fails, he should take another chance.
3. He is not such a man that he would tell a lie.
4. I do not know what is the name of this place.
5. As I was ill, I could not attend the class.
   [Or] I could not attend the class because I was ill.
6. When I went there, I found him ill.
7. He is working hard so that he can gain a prize.
8. He is so lazy that he cannot shine in life.
9. A moment that is lost is lost for ever.
10. As it is a day of strike, the children are playing on (in) the street.

11. The more you work hard, the more you succeed.
12. It was believed that he was very honest.
13. Do you wish that I should go?
14. They enquired why he failed.
15. Uneasy lies the head that wears the crown.
16. It was (such) a life that was hard enough.
17. They walked through the capital that was new.
18. They were so near death that they could see anything.
19. A stone that rolls gathers no moss.
    [Or] A stone that is rolling gathers no moss.
20. They need a lead that should be friendly.

EXERCISE 7

1. (i) He asked about the girl's stay.
   (ii) In modern life the rolling stone gathers the moss.
   (iii) The light load was too much for the old man.
   (iv) You need not ask my acquaintance.
   (v) A law cannot be passed without the assent of the Rashtrapati.
   (vi) The arguments on a decided matter are useless.
   (vii) I finish the letter for want of time.
   (viii) He had too little income to support his family.
   (ix) I shall buy it at any cost.
   (x) You are the first man to hear the news.
   (xi) He will not read the book wilfully.
   (xii) That is the burial place.
   (xiii) I have nothing to offer.
   (xiv) According to general belief, he died by poison.
   (xv) Their explanation cannot be true.
2. (i) Standing on the seashore in Puri we saw the waves rolling furiously.
   (ii) Darjeeling is one of the tea-producing areas of India.
   (iii) Being angry with me, he did not help me.
   (iv) Having finished his work, he left the room.
   (v) Being determined to oppose the bill, he stood up to speak.
3. (i) It is really wonderful to look at the shining stars in the sky.
   (ii) Though I have a leaden heart, yet I cannot help weeping.
   (iii) The scientists are recording the death pangs of a dying plant.
   (iv) Have you seen a fish flying in the sky?
   (v) Don't put your hand in boiling water.
   (vi) People living in glass-houses cannot afford throwing stones.

4. (i) Have you seen any weeping girl on the street?
   (ii) Milk is distributed to the customers in bottles which are sealed and sterilised.
   (iii) During sorting, the rotten oranges are thrown away.
   (iv) Mother asked Ayesha to iron the dried clothes.

EXERCISE 8

1. He went home and he was very happy to see his mother.
2. The rain stopped and they started for their destination.
3. He was (became) happy and agreed to a handsome donation.
4. He was old, but he carried a heavy load.
5. He picked up a ruler and hit the boy.
6. It was bad weather, still he scaled the mountain.
7. He is not only honest, but also sincere.
8. He took several efforts, yet he failed.
9. He must study hard, or he will not pass the examination.
10. He was ill, and so he could not attend the meeting.

EXERCISE 9

1. Not being abstract, you must be personal.
2. Its supreme virtue, not weakness is its familiarity.
3. Besides making a promise, he kept it.
4. The Spring came all over except the Giant's garden.
5. The soldier sank back on his seat in the moving train.
6. Setting his burden down with great gentleness, he sank upon the ground.
7. Coming back at the camp tonight, I'll write to everyone tomorrow.
8. Having not found the room suitable, Debu moved to the first floor.
9. We must not be late to avoid missing the bus.
10. Finding him guilty, the judge sentenced him to three years' imprisonment.

EXERCISE 10

1. Though he is rich, he is miserly.
2. Though he made several attempts, he failed.
3. Though he is outwardly strict, he is lenient at heart.
4. If we do not stand united and be divided, we fall.
   [Or] Unless we stand united and be divided, we fall.
5. If you spare the rod, you will spoil the child.
6. If you do not do, you will die./ If you do, you will not die.
7. If you study, you will learn.
8. If we take a few more attempts, we will succeed.
9. He is so weak that he cannot sit (up) on bed.
10. He is so ill that he is bound to lie in bed.

CHAPTER 28 : WH-QUESTIONS

EXERCISE A

1. When did the earthquake rock the city?
2. Who was in the room?
3. Where is logic in his statement?
4. Who does not love his motherland?
5. What is his address?
6. Why need I not pay the fees?
   [Or] Why am I not to pay the fees?
7. How fast does the train run?
8. How long did they wait for their friends?
9. What are you sure of?
10. When did they reach the place?
11. How many passengers were there in the bus?
12. What do the students aim at?
13. Whom does this book belong to?
14. Whose umbrella is this?
15. What is the next point?
16. When may such a happy day come again?
    [Or] When will such a happy day come?
17. Where can he be found out?
18. How could you be so rude?
19. When shall we see his like again?
20. Whom/Who are you speaking to?
21. How far is the market?
22. Where is sense in it?
23. What matters that we are not rich?
    [Or] What though we are not rich?
24. What is your opinion?
25. Who can conquer death?
26. Who could have done it?
27. What's the use of running so fast?
28. Who does not know that two and two make four?
29. How is your father?
30. What is his uncle?
31. How tall is the man?
32. How long is the track to run the race?
33. How often do you visit your friend's house?

34. Which saree did she purchase?
35. How does he usually go to school?
36. When did they make him the president?
37. Which school does he go to?
38. How long has the boy been working?
39. When can the glory of Shakespeare fade?
40. What made him leave the place?
41. When did I mention such a funny thing?
    [Or] When has such a funny thing been mentioned?
42. Which dishes does the girl prefer?
43. Whose book is this?
44. Which book is yours.

EXERCISE B

1. Who wrote 'Gulliver's Travels'?
2. Who is the author of 'Arms and the Man'?
3. Who is the writer of 'Pride and Prejudice'?
4. Which boy is the eldest brother?
5. Which book do you like to get?
6. What is your brother?
7. What are they waiting for?
8. What does he look like?
9. What for could he not attend the meeting?
   [Or] For what could he not attend the meeting?
10. What did he propose?
11. What's the time of departure of the train from Howrah?
12. What for have you come here?
    [Or] For what have you come here?
13. Why did they postpone the journey?
14. When did the students stand up?
15. How did he kill the wild boar?
16. How old is the smart young man?
17. Why could he not lift the load?
18. Whose house is it?
19. What did he seek in spite of knowing my difficulty?
20. How did he miss the train?
21. Why did he give up his study?
22. Which newspaper does she read daily?
23. Where did he come from Delhi?

24. What does the full moon look like?
25. What made you wake up?
26. How old is the smart young lady?
27. Why must we not waste time on reading trash?
28. What was the cause of the great commotion?
29. Why could he not reach the station in time?
30. What made him leave suddenly?
31. How did he break his leg?
32. Why could you not speak?
33. What prevented a serious accident?
34. Why could not your sister sit for the examination?
35. Who received the Oscar Award?
36. When did the boy break his leg?
37. How many people attended the meeting?
38. When will the solar eclipse occur?
39. What is the yardstick of judgement for calling an 'outsider'?
40. How often does he come here?
41. What made him give up sports?
42. Whom does Rahul love dearly?
43. Which chapter of the book do you prefer?
44. How fast does the train run?
45. When does he read (study) English?
46. Where did it occur?
47. How could you help me?
48. Whose pens are these?
49. How soon is he expected to come?
50. What time does the train leave Howrah?
51. What is your friend?
52. Why does he like to change his service?
53. What did they talk about so wistfully?
54. Where does the stranger come from?
55. How did the scholar win the gold medal?
56. Why did the teacher leave the class in rage?
57. When can Tagore's glory fade?
58. What prevented him from doing the work?
59. Where does the difference begin?
60. How was the disease cured?
61. When did the earthquake rock the city?

62. Whom did they invite to preside over the meeting?
63. Why could he not pass the examination?
64. How are you going on with the new washing machine?
    [Or] How is the new washing machine going on?
65. What caused great excitement among them?
66. What's the time please?
67. Who knows that you are a student?
    [Or] Who are you?
68. Whom did you see lying on the large mud floor?
69. What did he fail for in the examination?
    [Or] For what did he fail in the examination?
70. How many mangoes (on the table) did he eat?
71. Whose house is on the top of the hill?
72. What is this tool used for?
73. Why has a price been put on his head?
74. How does he disturb others' sleep?
75. Why were they bound to break the journey?
76. How did (could) China bag many Olympic Gold Medals?
77. When was the theft committed?
78. What is this cup made of?
79. Which are your books?/Which books are yours?
80. Where is the Cape of Good Hope?
81. When does the boy take exercise?
82. How long has he been working?
83. What is your brother?
84. Who is the author of 'As you Like It'?
85. How far is the market?
86. Why do you suffer much?
    [Or] Why do we suffer much for nothing?
87. How long can he read at a stretch?
88. Whose house is this?
89. Why was he kept indoors all day long?
90. Who was the first man to land on the moon?
91. What made him go to his friend's house?
92. What did Bibhas achieve?
    [Or] What for Bibhas achieved great success?
93. What is a world-famous Greek epic?
94. What brought Tagore the Nobel Prize?

95. What brought the farmer success in producing plenty of wheat?
96. Which discipline Kanika excels in?
97. How did the driver meet with an accident?
98. For what (What for) did Maradona's fans go into raptures over him?
99. How did Kapil Dev score a century?
100. What caused devastation in South-East Asia?

CHAPTER 29 : FORMATION OF WORDS/ANTONYMS

EXERCISE 1

(i) illegal, (ii) abuse, (iii) account, (iv) autograph, (v) contradiction, (vi) irregular, (vii) dishonour, (viii) ex-student, (ix) impossible, (x) inactive, (xi) antidote, (xii) ante-chamber.

EXERCISE 2

(i) beggar, (ii) speaker, (iii) typist, (iv) carrier/carriage, (v) absentee, absence, (vi) presentation, (vii) sailor, (viii) arrival, (ix) translation, (x) childhood, (xi) merriment, (xii) ability, (xiii) happiness. (xiv) brotherhood.

EXERCISE 3

(i) unable, (ii) inactive, (iii) below, (iv) careless, (v) uncommon, (vi) unconscious, (vii) discomfort, (viii) misconduct, (ix) misfortune, (x) dishonest, (xi) illegal, (xii) illiterate, (xiii) immoral. (xiv) immature, (xv) immature, (xvi) malpractice, (xvii) irregular, (xviii) unuseful, (xix) non-violence, (xx) invisible.

EXERCISE 4

(i) philatelist, (ii) oculist, (iii) surgeon, (iv) usurer, (v) curator, (vi) Mayor, (vii) malinger, (viii) optimist, (ix) pessimist, (x) patriot, (xi) pilgrim, (xii) prophet, soothsayer, (xiii) alien, emigrant, (xiv) delegate, (xv) intruder, trespasser, (xvi) traitor, (xvii) contemporary, (xviii) refugee, (xix) truant, (xx) amphibian.

CHAPTER 30 : WORD-FAMILY FROM ONE PART OF SPEECH TO OTHERS

EXERCISE 1

(i) Angry : He is an angry young man.
(ii) Beautify : She tries to beautify her face.
(iii) Central : This is the central part of the town.
(iv) Criminal : He is engaged in criminal activities.
(v) Dangerous : This part of the jungle is dangerous.
(vi) Dutiful : He is a dutiful man.
(vii) Dramatically : The whole thing was done dramatically.
(viii) Educate : It is our duty to educate our young ones.
(ix) Fearfully : She did the work fearfully.
(x) Fool, Befool : You cannot befool (fool) all the people.

(xi) Forcefully : The robbers entered the room forcefully.
(xii) Glorious : It was a glorious victory.
(xiii) Gracefully : She received the visitors gracefully.
(xiv) habitual : He is a habitual thief/liar.
(xv) Honourable : He is an honourable man in the locality.
(xvi) Horrible : The girl could not bear the horrible scene.
(xvii) Horrible : She said this humorously.
(xviii) Lawful : They will take lawful measures.
(xix) Valuable : Please give your valuable advice.
(xx) Wisdom : His wisdom is beyond question.

EXERCISE 2

(a) It was a memorable day when Independence was won.
(b) He follows blindly what others do.
(c) The child was under bad influences during the formative period of his life.
(d) Men may die, but this works are not destroyed.
(e) After months of negotiation, the two sides have been quietened and pleased.
(f) The manager/management is trying to reach an agreement with several separate unions.
(g) A passage of descriptive writing is very difficult to summarise.

EXERCISE 3

Whether viewing as a river or worshipping as a goddess, the Ganges occupies an important position in Hindu mythology. While the Rigveda mentions the Ganges only once, the later texts grow increasingly eloquent about it. It flows across he whole country and ultimately mingles in the Bay of Bengal. The water of the Ganges is supposed to be holy, although the degree of its pollution is very high.

CHAPTER 31 : SAME WORD USED AS DIFFERENT PARTS OF SPEECH

EXERCISE A

1. right—adjective, right—adjective. 2. much—adjective 3. much—adverb 4. little—adverb 5. little—adverb 6. little—adjective 7. loud—adjective 8. loud—adverb 9. hard—(predicative) adjective 10. hard—(predicative) adjective 11. hard—adverb 12. some—adverb 13. some—noun 14. early—adverb 15. early—adjective 16. all—pronoun 17. all—pronoun 18. all—adverb 19. best—adverb 20. best—adverb 21. best— adjective 22. but—adverb 23. but—(except) preposition (used at first for emphasis) 24. but—conjunction 25. but—adverb.

EXERCISE B

(i) Above (noun) : Our blessing comes from above.
(ii) Above (Preposition) : The moral law is above the civil laws.
(iii) After (Adverb) : After a while we started our journey.
(iv) After (Conjunction) : The doctor came after the patient had died.
(v) Better (Adjective) : I think yours is a better plan.
(vi) Better (Adverb) : I know him better.
(vii) Down (Noun) : There are ups and downs of (in) life.
(viii) Down (Adverb) : Down went the ship./The ball rolled down.
(ix) Head (Noun) : He is carrying a load on his head.
(x) Head (Verb) : He headed the ball in right time.
(xi) Honour (Noun) : He is a man of great honour.
(xii) Honour (Verb) : Everybody honours him./He is honoured by all.
(xiii) Little (Adjective) ; A little learning is a dangerous thing.
(xiv) Little (Adverb) : She eats very little.
(xv) Much (Adjective) : There is much sense in what he says.
(xvi) Much (Adverb) : Don't boast too much.
(xvii) Right (Noun) : It is a matter of right.
(xviii) Right (Adverb) : Serve him right.
(xix) Well (Adjective) : I am well. (Predicative Adjective).
(xx) Well (Adverb) : They played well.

CHAPTER 32 : WORDS COMMONLY CONFUSED

EXERCISE 1

[1] Accept [agree to take] : Accept the proposal.
Except [besides/excluding] : All except you are guilty.
[2] Access [a way of approaching] : There is no easy access to success.
Excess [amount beyond due] : I shall not give you any excess payment.
[3] Adapt [alter to suit] : Try to adapt to the new customs.
Adopt [take into a relationship] : Mr. Roy adopted an orphan as his son.
[4] Advice [counsel as a noun] : Listen to my advice.
Advise [give advice—as a verb] : The teacher advised the students.
[5] Affect [act badly] : Smoking affects health.
Effect [result] : What is the effect of such bad habit?
[6] Altar [a raised holy structure] : An altar has been made for the goddess.
Alter [change} : I have altered my plan.
[7] Bath [bathing—as a noun] : You should have a bath regularly.
Bathe [take a bath—as a verb] : He is bathing in a pond.

[8] Beside [on the side] : His house is beside the post office.
Besides [except] : Do you play any other game besides footballs?

[9] Cast [throw] : Cast your vote.
Caste [a unit of social division] : Caste is no bar to success.

[10] Career [a profession; progress through life] : Try to build your career.
Carrier [one who carries something; a support for luggage]: The mosquito is the carrier of malaria./My bike has a carrier.

[11] Cite [mention as an example] : He cited an example.
Site [the place of building or an event] : This is the site for the hospital.

[12] Cease [come to an end] : The factory ceased to work.
Seize [take hold of a thing forcibly or by legal right] : All the goods have been seized.

[13] Crops [the produce of fields] : The farmer is reaping the crops.
Corpse [a dead body] : Corpses are either burnt or buried.

[14] Complement [the word(s) to complete the predicate] : Some verbs take complements.
Compliment [praise/formal greetings/a gift] : A good work deserves compliment./Please pay my compliments to your parents.

[15] Council [a body to organize something] : He has applied to the H. S. Council.
Counsel [advice or to advise] : You need a good counsel.

[16] Credible [believable] : He is not at all credible.
Creditable [deserving praise] : He has achieved a creditable career.

[17] Decease [death or die] : The deceased person has no heir.
Disease [illness] : Cancer is a fatal disease.

[18] Defer [withhold] : The resolution was deferred.
Differ [disagree/be unlike] : I differ from you on this point.

[19] Die [cease to live] : The soldier died for the country.
Dye [colour, esp. by dipping in a liquid] : He is dyeing the cloth.

[20] Dew [tiny drop of condensed moisture] : The day passed like a dewdrop.
Due [payable/proper] : He came in due time to pay his dues.

[21] Eligible [regarded as suitable] : You are eligible for the post.
Illegible [not legible/hard to read] : His handwriting is illegible.

[22] Emigrant [a person who leaves his own country to settle in another] : He is an emigrant from India to Bangladesh.
Immigrant [a foreigner who comes into a country to live there] : He is an Indian immigrant in the USA.

[23] Expand [spread out] : A metal expands when it is heated.
Expend [spend] : You should not expend beyond your limit.

[24] Farther [Comp. of far] : Mumbai is farther from Delhi than Varanasi.
Further [additionally; more] : Prices are increasing further.

[25] Fair [beautiful/an exhibition for sale of goods]: She is a fair lady/The book fair is a fair for a fair cause.
Fare [the price of passage] : Ho much is the bus fare?

[26] Jealous [dubious about a rival] : Don't be jealous of your rival.
Zealous [enthusiastic] : He is a zealous worker.

[27] Loose [not rigidly fixed./untie] : A loose screw caused the accident./ Loose your belt before eating.
Lose [miss; be deprived of something] : He is losing his hair./Don't lose your confidence.

[28] Personal [individual]: It is my personal matter.
Personnel [persons employed in any service] : I need any of the electoral personnel.

[29] Peace [a state of harmony] : Let me die in peace.
Piece [one of the portions of a thing] : Please give me a piece of bread.

[30] Popular [liked by the people] : He is a popular teacher.
Populous [densely populated] : Kolkata is a populous city.

[31] Practice [the habit of doing anything] : Spitting is a bad practice.
Practise [habituate/use] : You shoud practise what you preach.

[32] Soldier [a fighting man in an army] : He is a brave soldier.
Shoulder [the junction of the body with the forelimb/assume responsibility] : He shoulders the burden on his broad shoulders.

[33] Stair [a single step on a series of steps] : Step on the stair of the staircase.
Stare [gaze at] : He stared hard at the knave.

[34] Steal [take other person's things secretly] : To steal is a crime.
Steel [hardened and refined iron] : This is made of steel.

[35] Tail [the hindermost hanging part of an animal] : Don't pull the tail of a dog.
Tale [a narrative or a story] : It is a tale of a greedy dog.

[36] Voluntary [subject to one's free will] : This is a voluntary job.
Volunteer [one who serves voluntarily or offers service voluntarily] : The volunteers should work properly./He volunteered his service in the project.

[37] Way [a path or road] : Could you tell me the way to the post office?
Weigh [to measure the weight] : This load should be weighed.

[38] Wave [swell on the surface of water] : The waves of the river rolled on the bank.
Waive [forgo] : The Employment Exchange waived the age-limit.

[39] Weak [not strong] : The old man is too weak to walk.
Week [a period of seven days] : Please come once a week.

[40] Warm [moderately hot/hearty] : Get warm by the fire./They gave him a warm reception.
Worm [a tiny insect] : The worm has consumed the book.

EXERCISE 2

[1] Admit [approve/allow] : I admit your claim.
Confess [express one's blame] : He confessed his guilt.

[2] Adapt [alter to suit] : This play has been adapted from the French edition.
Adept [skilful] : He is not adept in painting.
Adopt [choose, and take into a relationship] : They adopted an orphan.

[3] Affect [act badly or harmfully] : The building was badly affected by the fire.
Effect [consequence/reaction] : This medicine had no effect on the patient.

[4] Brake [a device for checking or check the motion of wheels, etc.] : The driver applied the brake to stop the car./He braked the car suddenly.
Break [separate into parts/make fracture] : She broke her leg./Glass breaks easily.

[5] Climate [overall long-term atmosphere] : The climate of India is hotter than that of England.
Weather [the state of short-term atmosphere for a particular period] : Do not go out in such foul weather.

[6] Complement [the word(s) added to complete the predicate] : An Intransitive verb may take a complement.
Compliment [praise/greeting/gift] : You deserve compliments./ Please pay my compliments to your parents.

[7] Habit [settled practice of an individual] : Give up your bad habit.
Custom [long-established practice in a society] : Dowry is an evil custom.

[8] Later [comparative of 'late'] : You may come later on./This is the later edition of the book.
Latter [last mentioned] : Between the two boys the former is strong, and the latter is weak.

[9] Latest [superlative of 'late'] : Come on Sunday at the latest./This the latest edition of the book.
Last [final/the end position] : December is the last month of the year./ This is the last piece of the cake.

[10] Tasteful [showing good taste] : The room is tastefully decorated.
Tasty [relishing] : This dish of meat is very tasty.

CHAPTER 33 : GROUP VERBS/PHRASAL VERBS

EXERCISE A

[1] They talked over the meeting.
[2] The meeting was put off.
[3] The two boys fell out over the purse.
[4] He will soon get over the difficulties.
[5] You should not look down upon the poor.
[6] Lila came across her old friend.
[7] The patient passed ways peacefully.
[8] The price of rice is going down.
[9] He has borne away the first prize.
[10] The strike was called off.
[11] The light has been put out.
[12] He set out for Paris.
[13] He gets up early in the morning.
[14] He called on me in my office.
[15] You should not run into debts.
[16] Our school breaks up at 4 pm.
[17] The rains have set in.
[18] He dealt with me very well.
[19] Have you come by an article?
[20] It came about in this way.
[21] I have gone through the book.
[22] Try to look up the word in the dictionary.
[23] I have looked into the matter carefully.
[24] I have made out your words.
[25] Please go on with your studies.
[26] He laid by something for his old age.
[27] Moher looked after her child.
[28] He passes for a great scholar.
[29] She takes after her mother.
[30] I have asked for his explanation.

EXERCISE B

[1] He put off his shoes before entering his house.

[2] Overwork has told upon his health.

[3] The boys and girls got into the carriage.

[4] The robbers broke into the house.

[5] I can work out the problem easily.

[6] I cannot put up with such an insult.

[7] He is passed for a scholar.

[8] The villagers ran after the thief.

[9] The patient will soon come round.

[10] The President gave away the prizes.

[11] You should keep down your anger.

[12] Try to keep up your reputation.

[13] Don't fall out with your brother.

[14] I cannot call up your name.

[15] I will soon get over my difficulties

EXERCISE C

Mr Roy deals in umbrella, but he does not deal well with his customers. Our school breaks up at 4 pm. Overwork tells upon his health. We should not look down upon the poor. His proposal was turned down and he was turned away of the room. Try to work out the sum.

EXERCISE D

[1] Hi health has broken down for hard labour.

[2] You should give up your bad habit.

[3] There is none to look after the orphan.

[4] Such hard work will act upon your health.

[5] The patient will come round soon.

[6] Don't fall out with your friend.

[7] Try to lay by something for bad days.

[8] The student could not make out what the teacher said.

[9] He could not work out the sum.

[10] At last the strike was called off.

CHAPTER 34 : PHRASES AND IDIOMS

EXERCISE A

[1] **ABC** [primary knowledge] : He does not know even the ABC of music.

[2] **Above board** [beyond doubt] : His activities are above board.

[3] **Bad blood** [ill-feeling] : Now there is no bad blood between the two brothers.

[4] **Black sheep** [a bad character] : He is a black sheep in the family.

[5] **Big gun** [a leading person] : He is a big gun in our society.

[6] **Curry favour** [be favourite through flattery] : He knows how to curry favour with his loss.

[7] **Die in harness** [die while in service] : Mr. Mitra died in harness.

[8] **End in smoke** [fail] : All his plans ended in smoke.

[9] **Fight shy** [avoid] : Why do you fight shy of me?

[10] **Gala day** [a day of festivity] : The 'Id' is a gala day to the Muslims.

[11] **Hush money** [bribe money] : He offered some hush money to the officer.

[12] **Irony of fate** [bad luck] : He could not succeed in the final round by irony of fate.

[13] **Lame excuse** [weak plea] : They will not accept any lame excuse.

[14] **Man of letters** [a scholar] : Undoubtedly he was a man of letters.

[15] **Moot point** [an important undecided matter] : To accept cloaning is still a moot point in science.

[16] **Null and void** [invalid] : The decree has been null and void in the High Court.

[17] **Out of date** [out of fashion] : This fashion is now out of date.

[18] **Pros and cons** [details] : You should consider the pros and cons of the problem.

[19] **Ups and downs** [rise and fall] : There are ups and downs in our life.

[20] **White elephant** [a costly but unprofitable undertaking] : Some say that the post of a Governor in our States is a white elephant.

EXERCISE B

[1] His activities are above board.

[2] The paternal property is the apple of discord among the brothers.

[3] The sun is, as it were, the lamp of the universe.

[4] His popularity is at a low ebb/on the wane.

[5] The two brothers are now at daggers drawn.

[6] He feels at home at his friend's house.

[7] He is at home in mathematics.

[8] He is beating the bush at random.

[9] He reached there at the eleventh hour.

[10] He left the place bag and baggage.
[11] The beauty of the Taj beggars description.
[12] He will come here by and by.
[13] Lila dances by fits and starts/off and on.
[14] The price of rice is increasing by leaps and bounds.
[15] The dowry system is the burning question newadays.
[16] Mass education is the crying need of India.
[17] I do not know why he fights shy of me.
[18] Nobody can believe such a cock and bull story.
[19] Tell me the story in a nutshell.
[20] He comes here off and on.

CHAPTER 35 : NOMINAL COMPOUNDS

EXERCISE 1

(a) stone wall, (b) labour-saving method, (c) machine cloth, (d) mountain streams, (e) TV serial, (f) radio programme, (g) footpath, (h) toy train, (i) sportsman, (j) birthday party, (k) census report.

EXERCISE 2

(a) textile of jute, (b) a fan hanging from ceiling, (c) a spoon for stirring tea, (d) a pan for buying food, (e) a stove lit by gas, (f) a pool for swimming, (g) a friend cherished in bosom, (h) a fiction on science, (i) gas causing tears, (j) a producer of film, (k) a police to control traffic, (l) a fair to display and sell books, (m) countries that produce wheat, (n) a system that controls aircraft.

EXERCISE 3

(a) He is an excellent bookbinder.
(b) There is a lot of books on the book-shelf.
(c) The price of gas cylinder is rising high.
(d) The importance of cottage industry cannot be neglected.
(e) You should be aware of poison gas.
(f) The government should take care of the tea gardens.
(g) She/He is a heart-throbbing film star.
(h) That lady is a telephone operator.
(i) You must come to my birthday party.
(j) The bus owners are demanding to rise bus fare.
(k) When do you take your breakfast usually?

EXERCISE 4

(a) Have you ever seen a flying-fish?

(b) A well-fed child will be healthy.

(c) The angel saw the dead swallow in the dustheap.

(d) The withered violate lay on the table.

(e) It is a dining table.

(f) When a little poison is added, the plant shows its shuddering reaction.

EXERCISE 5

(a) These mountain streams are flowing into the sea.

(b) Bring me the icebag.

(c) This is a windmill.

(d) The children are riding a toy train.

(e) Go to the bedroom.

(f) We should give due importance on cottage industries.

(g) He deserves praise as a tax-payer.

(h) The man is a famous snake-charmer.

CHAPTER 36 : PUNCTUATION AND CAPITALIZATION EXERCISE

(a) "He is too foolish," she said.

(b) Uncle Podger said, "Do you think I am a fool?"

(c) She said, "Sweet my child, I live for thee."

(d) I had it in my hand a minute ago.

(e) "This is a delightful spot," he said, "we must ask the Hail on a visit."

(f) The second cricket match between India and England started at Eden Gardens on 31st December.

(g) On the first day India won the toss and decided to bat. The opening batsman batted well, but England bowled very well also.

(h) The weather was not good on the second day. The game had to be stopped before time. The Indian batsmen were batting very well, and they had already scored a good total.

(i) The game was a very slow one on the third day, and cricket-lovers were unhappy. They wanted good cricket.

(j) The soyabean is a plant with great food value, but neither the farmers nor the common people knew very much about it.

(k) We can either drink milk or use it for making tea, coffee and other drinks. Other milk products are sandesh, pudding, and dahi.

(l) The Soviet Union and the United States have made great progress in exploring outer space. The USSR was the first to launch a satellite.

(m) Who's there ? Who's there, I say? Am I to get no sleep tonight?

(n) "How did you get here, child? Whose baby are you?" The man asked.

(o) The convict said, "They have made me a thief. God curse them all !"

(p) Hallo, Mr crocodile! Why are you lying in the sun? Aren't you feeling hot?

(q) Boys! You know the need for planting trees. We want to start a tree-planting project.

(r) The boys turned up the soil and added fertiliser after they had planted the saplings and watered them well.

(s) With which game are Sourav Ganguli and Sachin Tendulkar associated?

(t) How do you greet your teacher when he enters the class in the morning?

(u) What is the most important quality of a student?

(v) How many members are there in your family? Who are they? Please introduce them.

(w) Suddenly I heard a howl just behind me. My cousin cried out, "Help! Help!"

(x) We saw the thief being chased by the guards. They caught the thief and beat him badly.

(y) The Wind was very angry. He said to the Sun, "Men always prefer you to me; that is why you have succeeded."

(z) The Sun smiled and said, "No, Mr Jealous! I am really stronger than you are though I never brag. Men like good behaviour most, so I am successful."

CHAPTER 37 : COMMON ERRORS/CORRECT USAGE

EXERCISE A

1. He advises me to wait.
2. I am senior to him.
3. You are junior to him.
4. This book is preferable to that.
5. Your information is false.

6. I will inform your father.
7. The rain stopped yesterday.
8. I am confident of winning.
9. This tea is preferable to that.
10. One ought to love one's country.
11. A number of boys have come.
12. He is an M.A./M.Sc.
13. The Ganga is a sacred river.
14. Where are you going?
15. He is taller than his sister.
16. The scenery of the hillside is lovely.
17. He passed last year.
18. He said that he would go after a week.
19. He speaks English fluently.
20. It is a unique thing.
21. She resembles my daughter.
22. Five rupees is a small sum.
23. He gave me the book I wanted.
24. She availed herself of the offer.
25. He as well as I is guilty.
26. Either you or I am wrong.
27. I know how to speak English.
28. He is taller than she.
29. He delivered (made) a good speech.
30. His health is very good.
31. Do not tell a lie.
32. Man is mortal.

EXERCISE B

1. He told me this.
2. I passed my driving test.

3. I believe in God.
4. He called me a fool.
5. Let me write with a pen.
6. He gave the most perfect answer.
7. He is better (comparatively good) today.
8. This mango tastes sweet.
9. I rang (have rung) the bell.
10. He wrote a good book.
11. He does not know how to swim.
12. He is ill for a week.
13. Debu said that he would do it.
14. He came here yesterday.
15. He is my cousin.
16. He and I are neighbours.
17. Tell/Recite the poem from heart.
18. Man is mortal.
19. He is a European.
20. Gold is yellow.
21. Tell me what your name is.
22. He prevents me from going there.
23. He is the worst student in the class.
24. Sunil is an NCC cadet.
25. Does he speak English?
26. He was hanged for murder.
27. He died yesterday.
28. We had a picnic yesterday./We shall have a picnic tomorrow.
29. Columbus discovered America.
30. All the furniture were lost.

31. Physics is not easy to learn.
32. He is better between the two boys./He is the best of the boys.
33. Each of the students was punished.
34. Any of the three teams might win.
35. Either he or I am to blame.
36. We read grammar with the Headmaster.

CHAPTER 38 : FIGURES OF SPEECH

EXERCISE A

1. Childhood is like a passing dream.—Simile
2. Variety is the spice of life.—Metaphor
3. Truth sits upon the dying man.—Personification
4. There is dagger in thy words.—Metaphor
5. He is a man of iron will.—Metaphor
6. Swiftly flies the feathered death.—Personification
7. The more haste, the less speed.—Paradox
8. Rana Pratap was the lion of India.—Metaphor
9. Hitler's mad policy let lose the dogs of war.—Metaphor
10. The soldiers were swifter than eagles and stronger than lions.—Hyperbole
11. The chair collapsed under the weight of the philosopher.—Irony
12. The midday sun is a mystic dog with paws of fire.—Metaphor/Allegory
13. A thousand years are as yesterday where it is lost.—Hyperbole
14. Hope is the poor man's bread.—Metaphor
15. Poverty is a blessing in a good many situations.—Paradox
16. In the large family he had many mouths to feed.—Synecdoche
17. How sweet the moonlight sleeps upon this bank!—Personification/Exclamation
18. Sweet are the uses of adversity.—Oxymoron

19. Speech was given to man to conceal his thoughts.—Paradox
20. They speak like saints, and act like devils.—Antithesis

EXERCISE B

1. The man is as busy as a bee.
2. The boy is as cheerful as a lark.
3. He is as clever as a crow.
4. He is as cunning as a fox.
5. The beggar is as dirty as a hog.
6. He remained as dumb as a statue.
7. He ran as fast as a hare.
8. You are growing as fat as a pig.
9. The boy is as gentle as a lamb.
10. The man is as greedy as a wolf.
11. This metal is as hard as stone.
12. He is as hungry as a hawk.
13. This ornament is as light as a feather.
14. His voice was as loud as thunder.
15. She remains as mute as a fish.
16. She is as nervous as a mouse.
17. The pyramid is as old as the hills.
18. He is as proud as a peacock.
19. He looks as ugly as a toad.
20. The old man is as wise as a judge.